THE
WESTMORLAND
WAY

HILLSIDE GUIDES
by the same author

THE
WESTMORLAND
WAY

by

Paul Hannon

HILLSIDE PUBLICATIONS

HILLSIDE PUBLICATIONS
11 Nessfield Grove
Exley Head
Keighley
West Yorkshire
BD22 6NU

First published 1983
Revised and reprinted 1986

To the inspiration of
an **A**dopted **W**estmerian

Cover illustration: looking up Ullswater from Bonscale Pike
Page 7 : detail from the memorial to Lady Anne
Clifford in St. Lawrence's, Appleby

ISBN   0 9509212 5 4

Printed in Great Britain by
Carnmor Print and Design
95/97 London Road
Preston
Lancashire
PR1 4BA

CONTENTS

Ormside Hall, from the church

Appleby

Arnside

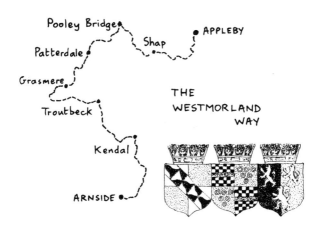

INTRODUCTION

The Westmorland Way is a 98-mile walk through the old county of that name, which as we all know and a good many regret, disappeared in 1974 at the hands of the bureaucrats hidden in Whitehall. If Westmorland has been ruthlessly wiped off the map, it's name has been preserved in many forms, and this effort is one further contribution to that memory.

The story of this walk began in 1977, when as a result of completing the Coast to Coast walk, the author took a leaf out of A. Wainwright's book and took up his suggestion of planning one's own long-distance walk. The Way was walked for the first time at Easter 1982, and these pages contain the end result.

The book is presented in a style familiar to all walkers on these northern hills: though not quite Wainwright class, no apologies are offered for adopting his format. His methods are quite simply the best.

The Westmorland Way has been joined by two companion guides (see pages 92 and 93) to form a magnificent 250-mile circuit of the Lakes Counties.

The walk itself, as the name suggests, stretches across Westmorland in the shape roughly of a large loop, and it remains entirely within the county boundary. To avoid the walk being conducted like a postmortem, all references to Westmorland will be made in the present tense.

Appleby, Westmorland's county town provides the starting point in the shadow of the Pennine Chain, and the walk finishes on the shores of

Morecambe Bay at Westmorland's only port, Arnside. In between, a superb cross-section of the county's delights is encountered, as the Way moves from the Pennines to the sea by way of riverbank, farmland, fellside, village, lakeshore, towpath and mountain top.

Bowfell
from above Thrang quarry

The route follows public rights-of-way and as far as is known commits no trespass. Although some stretches of path may have been linked by quiet lanes giving pleasant walking, all main roads have been generally avoided : where they are met they are left almost as quickly, and nowhere is heavy traffic met without the accompaniment of a footpath alongside.

The planned duration of the walk is seven days, thus allowing it to be completed in a single week's holiday. The book has therefore been divided into seven sections : each describes a reasonable day's walking and each has accommodation at the end of the day, without the need to stray far off-route in search of it.

The Shelter, Scout Scar

All eight of the suggested overnight halts, from Appleby to Arnside inclusive, provide a fairly good choice of lodgings of varying degrees of luxury. Each has hotel and bed-and-breakfast facilities and youth hostels are particularly well-sited. They can be found at Dufton (two miles from Appleby), Patterdale, Grasmere (two), Troutbeck (listed as Windermere), Kendal and at Arnside. There are two further hostels which are on the route but not at the recommended halts: these are Elterwater and Ambleside.

It goes without saying that the Way could alternatively be completed in a series of separate day walks.

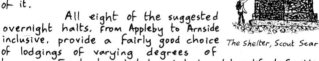

The Westmorland Way —
in relation to the counties of Westmorland and it's neighbours

Surely the least spoilt and overall the most scenic county in England, Westmorland is fairly well self-contained, for it has mostly mountainous borders with all but one of it's neighbours. The exception is Lancashire, which in it's two separate parts (the Furness area is completely detached) provides a cushion between the hills and the county's tiny seaboard on Morecambe Bay.

It should be stressed that at almost any time between Easter and Autumn accommodation may be hard to find in the popular centres (i.e. those within the National Park) and really do need to be booked in advance. The youth hostels in particular are prone to heavy occupation by school parties at certain times.

The only transport required should be that to and from the terminal points. Fortunately, and amazingly even, both Appleby and Arnside are endowed with their own railway stations. Both are in interesting railway country, for Appleby is astride that most majestic of lines, the Settle-Carlisle, while Arnside is at the start of the scenic line round Furness and the Cumbrian coast, and is also only a few miles from the Steamtown railway museum at Carnforth. For anyone with a fear of trains, both places can also be reached by bus, most easily from Penrith and Kendal respectively.

A related interest of many walkers is that of seeking out suitable refreshment either during or after a day's walking. The only beer worth spending one's hard-earned money on is traditional ale, and the walker who prefers the real thing is adequately catered for on this walk. In order not to become

Patterdale

a pub-guide, individual places are not listed here, but anyone with a keen enough interest can always obtain further information.

As an appetiser, below is a list of breweries that supply traditional beer to some or all of their outlets on the Westmorland Way. The fact that details can change rapidly is emphasised by the realisation that two breweries in the first edition of this guide do not exist any longer: it's likely more will soon follow them.

Bass, Burton and Tadcaster	Theakston, Masham and Carlisle
Hartley, Ulverston	Thwaites, Blackburn
Jennings, Cockermouth	Vaux, Sunderland
Lorimer, Edinburgh	Whitbread, Salford and Co. Durham
Marston, Burton	Wilson, Manchester
Tetley Walker, Warrington	Younger, Edinburgh

The Westmorland Way – physical features

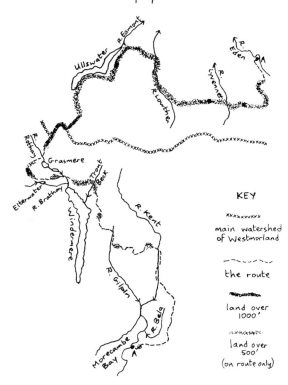

KEY

xxxxxxxxxx

main watershed
of Westmorland

- - - - - - -

the route

land over
1000'

land over
500'
(on route only)

The main watershed divides
the county from east to west: rivers in the northern
half all join the Eden to flow into the Solway Firth,
while those in the southern half find their way more
individually into Morecambe Bay. The two main rivers
Eden and Kent are accompanied for a time, each at
one extreme of the walk. England's two largest lakes
are also encountered: Windermere can be seen for
three days, while Ullswater is explored more intimately.

Ordnance Survey maps required

It is inconceivable to imagine completing any walk without the relevant O.S. maps, and this one is no exception: to obtain maximum enjoyment from the walk, they are as important as the guide itself.

1:50,000 metric scale

sheet 90: Penrith and Keswick
91: Appleby-in-Westmorland
97: Kendal

1 inch to the mile

sheet 83: Penrith
89: Lancaster and Kendal
Tourist Map of the Lake District

....

Market and Early Closing Days

	Market Day	Early closing
Appleby	Sat.	Thurs.
Shap	Mon.	Thurs./Sat.
Patterdale	/	Fri.
Grasmere	/	Thurs.
Ambleside	Weds.	Thurs.
Kendal	Sat.	Thurs.
Arnside	/	Thurs.

SOME USEFUL ADDRESSES

The Ramblers' Association
1/5 Wandsworth Road, London SW8 2LJ
Tel. 01- 582 6878

Youth Hostels Association
Trevelyan House, St. Albans, Herts. AL1 2DY
Tel. 0727 - 55215
Regional Office: Elleray, Windermere
Tel. Windermere (09662) 2301/2

Friends of the Lake District
Secretary: J. M. Houston, Gowan Knott, Kendal Rd,
Staveley, nr. Kendal LA8 9AP
Tel. Kendal (0539) 821201

Cumbria Tourist Board
Ashleigh, Windermere LA23 2AQ
Tel. Windermere (09662) 4444

The National Trust
36 Queen Anne's Gate, London SW1H 9AS
Tel. 01- 222 9251
Membership: P.O. Box 30, Beckenham, Kent BR3 4TL

Ribble Motor Services
Head office: Frenchwood Ave, Preston PR1 4LU
Tel. Preston (0772) 54754
Bus Station, Blackhall Road, Kendal
Tel. Kendal (0539) 20932

Mountain Goat Bus Company
Victoria Street, Windermere
Tel. Windermere (09662) 5161

Campaign For Real Ale
34 Alma Road, St. Albans, Herts AL1 3BW
Tel. St. Albans (0727) 67201

Lake District Weather Forecast
Tel. Windermere (09662) 5151

THE COUNTRY CODE

Respect the life and work of the countryside

Protect wildlife, plants and trees

Keep to public paths across farmland

Safeguard water supplies

Go carefully on country roads

Keep dogs under control

Guard against all risks of fire

Fasten all gates

Leave no litter - take it with you

Make no unnecessary noise

Leave livestock, crops and machinery alone

Use gates and stiles to cross fences, hedges and walls

THE ROUTE GUIDE

The maps in this guide take the form of one continuous strip-map, which is spread over all the right-hand pages (whilst occasionally overlapping onto the opposite left-hand page) from page 19 to page 85 inclusive. On the same or facing page will be found a detailed commentary on the route-maps that are depicted there. What space then remains is left to notes and drawings of the many features of interest along the way. Each daily section commences with an introductory page, which can be easily located by reference to the contents on page 5.

The strip-maps are all on the scale of 2'2 inches to one mile, and north is always at the top of the page.

key to the map symbols

Route — clear — sketchy — no path

Route on public road — unenclosed — wall — Fence/hedge

Contours — 700 — 800 (at intervals of 100 feet)

Railway line

Crags — Loose rock/scree — Limestone outcrop — Marsh — Trees

Buildings — Church — cairn (summit / other) — abbreviations
g – gate
s – stile
c – cattle grid

Miles from Appleby — (47)

Map continuation (indication page no) — 69

DAY ONE

APPLEBY TO SHAP

Distance — 16¾ miles

Going — easy

Highest point — Hardendale Nab, 1165 feet

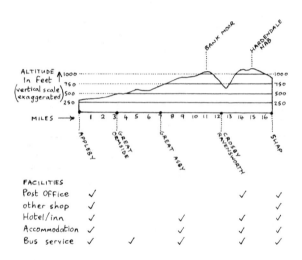

FACILITIES

	APPLEBY	GREAT ORMSIDE	GREAT ASBY	CROSBY RAVENSWORTH	SHAP
Post Office	✓			✓	✓
other shop	✓				✓
Hotel/inn	✓		✓	✓	✓
Accommodation	✓		✓	✓	✓
Bus service	✓	✓	✓	✓	✓

The first day of the walk begins under the Pennines and ends on the fringe of Lakeland. A riverside start is superceded by some fields and quiet lanes by way of Great Ormside and Rutter Force, before Great Asby is reached. By then the transition from sandstone to limestone is complete. This day's journey through the old style Westmorland continues over higher ground and open moor to Crosby Ravensworth via the old hall at Gaythorne, and to Shap via a stone circle and some typical limestone scenery.

Appleby-in-Westmorland

Appleby is a classic country town full of interest both ancient and modern. Until local government reorganisation Appleby proudly held the title of County Town of Westmorland, an honour bestowed on it long ago when it ranked of greater importance than Kendal. Indeed, Appleby seemed justified in its claim to have been Englands smallest county town. When the old county disappeared and took Applebys status with it, the town decided on a change of name to Appleby-in-Westmorland in order to preserve that particular link with the past.

It is the past that is much in evidence here, for the town is steeped in history. The 'piece de resistance' is undoubtedly the main street, known as Boroughgate, which extends from the Parish Church at one end to the Castle at the other, rising gradually the whole way. Boroughgate is exceptionally broad and is lined with beautiful trees and an interesting assortment of buildings. The castle does not dominate the town despite being in its rightful position at the top of the hill; in fact it remains rather aloof. Its best preserved portion is the Keep, and is open to visitors as a centre for the Rare Breeds Survival Trust.

Each end of Boroughgate is graced with a tall cross bearing a sundial; the one at the top is 17th century and divides the road in two, while the other, which is 18th century, stands in the centre of things in the Market Square.

Appleby:
The Market Place

Route

The footpath stays close to the fence and maintains it's height above the river to provide excellent views of the Westmorland Pennines to the east. When the path meets a fence running down to the river there is a fine prospect of the Ormside Viaduct, and it is here we say goodbye to the Eden which has given us such a good send-off. From the stile the path bears right to enter the wooded confines of Jeremy Gill via another stile.

Cross the footbridge and bear right up the opposite slope alongside a tributary of the main beck, which gives up the ghost by the time a gate is reached. From it follow a hedgerow on the left, leading to a track sloping up to the left between more leafy hedgerows. The railway soon appears ahead and when the hedgerow turns right, stay with it and use a stile to join a farm-lane. Accompany it under the railway bridge and it will lead unerringly onto the minor road at Great Ormside.

Turn right along the road, under another railway bridge and gradually up to a crossroads. Head straight across and up the lane as far as the isolated house on the left. Here take a stile by a gate on the right, and head half-left to a stile in the top corner. Keeping a fence on the left another stile is encountered before a gradual descent onto a lane. Turn left along it and then branch right on reaching a lane signposted to Rutter Force.

The River Eden first sees the light of day high on the lonely Mallerstang fells, only a mile from Yorkshire's border. It flows ever northward to empty into the Solway Firth near Carlisle, and at various stages receives every drop of water encountered in the next 3½ days. Our brief acquaintance with it is along a pleasant stretch with fine views of the Pennines.

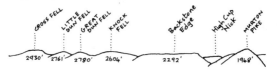

The North Pennines from above the River Eden

The RIVER EDEN to RUTTER FORCE

Great Ormside is a farming community standing peacefully above the River Eden. The tiny church is a gem: one of Westmorland's oldest, a substantial part dates back to Norman times. Dedicated to St. James, it overlooks the Eden from the top of a grassy knoll, actually an artificial mound of ancient origin. In the shadow of the church is Ormside Hall, now a farm, but incorporating a centuries-old wing. The impressive 10-arch Ormside Viaduct carries the famous Settle-Carlisle line over the river just to the north.

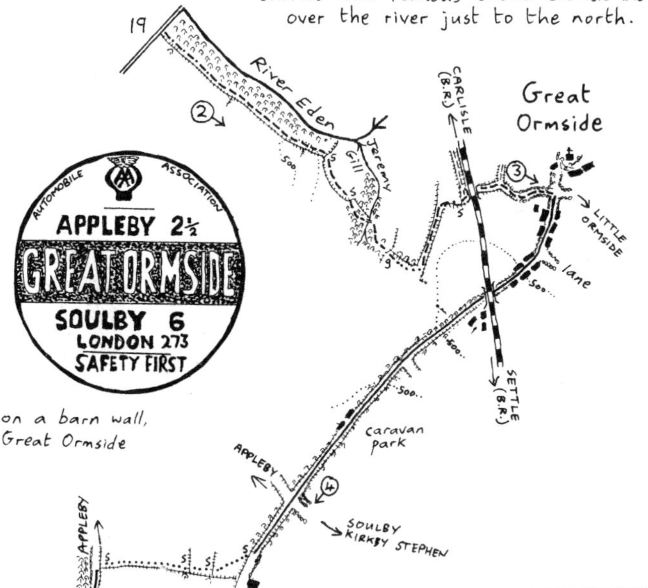

19
River Eden
2
Jeremy Gill
CARLISLE (B.R.)
Great Ormside
3
LITTLE ORMSIDE
lane
500
SETTLE (B.R.)
caravan park
APPLEBY
4
SOULBY
KIRKBY STEPHEN
APPLEBY
600
AUTOMOBILE ASSOCIATION
APPLEBY 2½
GREAT ORMSIDE
SOULBY 6
LONDON 273
SAFETY FIRST

on a barn wall, Great Ormside

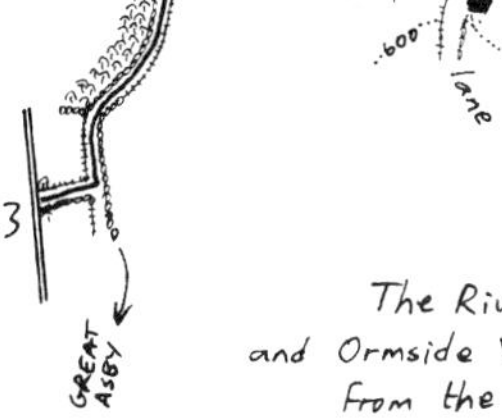

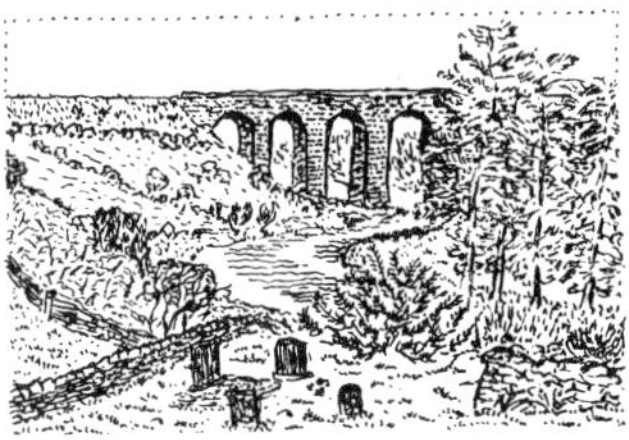

lane
23
GREAT ASBY

The River Eden and Ormside Viaduct from the church

Route

As the lane approaches the beck Rutter Force comes into view, and on arrival the grassy bank provides an obvious resting-place. Those still not bereft of childhood habits can paddle across the ford, the rest can use the footbridge to reach the far bank. Leave the lane almost immediately for a gate behind the cottage. Behind the old mill a stile is then reached in a fence adjacent to the top of the waterfall. Continue on through a gateway and then follow the beck as far as a wooden farm-bridge crossing. Having negotiated a gate at each side of the bridge, head up the field to a conspicuous row of trees: follow these to the right to meet a fence. Use a gate in it and turn immediately left to pass a small plantation before emerging onto a quiet lane via a stile. Turn right, past an isolated chapel, and remain on the lane for a quick mile's walking to arrive at a crossroads, across which Great Asby is soon entered.

Head up the main street, past the church to a junction of lanes by some open ground. Take the one turning sharp right, and stay on this tarmac farm-road as it passes through a field, over a bridge and past a barn to enter a large tract of rough pasture. Here the tarmac ends and the way forks: ignore the left branch which enters another field, and take the concrete track heading steeply up to the right. This well-surfaced farm road makes the going easy. After crossing a cattle-grid it resumes it's climb, and soon reaches another grid at the level approach to Halligill Farm. Here we abandon it: do not cross the grid but go straight ahead to a gate in a fence, then join a wall on the right to use a stile by the first gate reached. Head down the large field entered, bearing a little right to reach a stream along the bottom of it, at the edge of Halligill Wood.

St. Peter's, Great Asby

Halligill

25

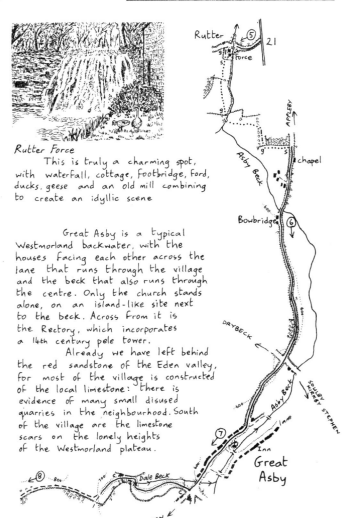

Rutter Force

Rutter Force

This is truly a charming spot, with waterfall, cottage, footbridge, ford, ducks, geese and an old mill combining to create an idyllic scene

Great Asby is a typical Westmorland backwater, with the houses facing each other across the lane that runs through the village and the beck that also runs through the centre. Only the church stands alone, on an island-like site next to the beck. Across from it is the Rectory, which incorporates a 14th century pele tower.

Already we have left behind the red sandstone of the Eden valley, for most of the village is constructed of the local limestone: there is evidence of many small disused quarries in the neighbourhood. South of the village are the limestone scars on the lonely heights of the Westmorland plateau.

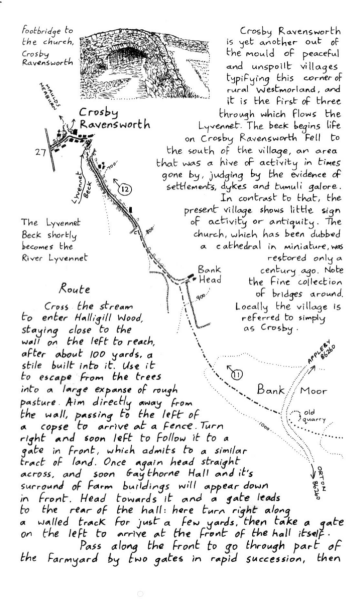

footbridge to
the church,
Crosby
Ravensworth

MAULDS MEABURN

Crosby
Ravensworth

27

Lyvennet Beck

100'

12

The Lyvennet
Beck shortly
becomes the
River Lyvennet

800'

Bank
Head

900'

Crosby Ravensworth
is yet another out of
the mould of peaceful
and unspoilt villages
typifying this corner of
rural Westmorland, and
it is the first of three
through which flows the
Lyvennet. The beck begins life
on Crosby Ravensworth Fell to
the south of the village, an area
that was a hive of activity in times
gone by, judging by the evidence of
settlements, dykes and tumuli galore.
In contrast to that, the
present village shows little sign
of activity or antiquity. The
church, which has been dubbed
a cathedral in miniature, was
restored only a
century ago. Note
the fine collection
of bridges around.
Locally the village is
referred to simply
as Crosby.

Route

Cross the stream
to enter Halligill Wood,
staying close to the
wall on the left to reach,
after about 100 yards, a
stile built into it. Use it
to escape from the trees
into a large expanse of rough
pasture. Aim directly away from
the wall, passing to the left of
a copse to arrive at a fence. Turn
right and soon left to follow it to a
gate in front, which admits to a similar
tract of land. Once again head straight
across, and soon Gaythorne Hall and it's
surround of farm buildings will appear down
in front. Head towards it and a gate leads
to the rear of the hall: here turn right along
a walled track for just a few yards, then take a gate
on the left to arrive at the front of the hall itself.
Pass along the front to go through part of
the farmyard by two gates in rapid succession, then

APPLEBY B6260

11

Bank Moor

old
quarry

1000'

ORTON B6260

HALLIGILL WOOD to CROSBY RAVENSWORTH

Route continued

continue on the same line along another walled farm-track which soon becomes tarmac. At a cattle-grid we emerge onto the open moor: here leave the farm-road and head up the slope to the right. Bear slightly left and as the gradient eases continue ahead to arrive at the Appleby-Orton road.

The road crosses Bank Moor at it's highest point, and here, opposite the extensive scars of an old quarry, the road is left in favour of a faint bridleway heading in a north-westerly direction. The short-cropped turf permits rapid progress and as the path swings right it meets an intake-wall leading to the farm of Bank Head. We merge into it's access road which leads all the way down to Crosby Ravensworth. Just short of the village leave it for a footbridge, from where a path winds round onto a back lane. Turn left to enter the village centre just opposite the church.

St. Patrick's, Crosby Ravensworth

Gaythorne Hall

Dating from the sixteenth century, this fine structure has a history containing macabre legends.

Route

Turn left along the main road through the village and leave it by a lane which starts opposite the village hall and is signposted to Shap. Initially very steep, the gradient eases as we pass the farms of Low and High Haiberwain to arrive at a sharp right-hand bend. Here leave the lane by taking the gate straight ahead, and continue in the same direction on a track alongside a plantation. Stay with the wall on the right to rise very gradually across the rough pasture, diverting a little to the left at the brow of the hill to visit the stone circle. Just by the wall itself note the ring of stones which mark the site of an earthwork, one of Crosby Ravensworth barrows.

Descend now, still by the wall, with extensive views of lakeland's eastern fells straight ahead. At a gate continue downhill on a wide grassy avenue between walls, to join a narrow lane. Cross the cattle-grid and head up the rough pasture opposite. Keep close by the wall on the left to pass over limestone pavements, then aim for the top corner of the pasture where a fence is overshadowed by a moonscape of quarry debris. From a gate at the right end of the fence follow a narrow strip of green between the quarry and a wall. The confines of the quarry are left in the same way, and from a gate head half-left onto an unenclosed road. Cross straight over and continue in the same direction to a gate set a good 50 yards back from the road. Head away to a stile in the next wall, continuing down to a footbridge over the motorway.

From it bear half-right to a stile, continuing across two more fields to join a walled track leading to a bridge over the railway.

From it descend to houses and out onto the main street.

For the half-mile between the motorway and Shap's main street, our route coincides with the Coast to Coast Walk.

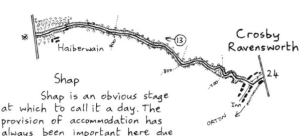

Shap

Shap is an obvious stage at which to call it a day. The provision of accommodation has always been important here due to it's lonely position on the A6, there being no other village on the 26-mile stretch between Kendal and Penrith. Although the motorway has put an end to the glory days, there are still many travellers passing through, not least because of another certain walk that makes use of Shap's most useful situation. To the south of the village the A6 reaches it's high point of 1397 feet, and calls to mind the days when the term 'going over Shap' was much used. In railway terms Shap is also well-known, the famous Shap Summit is reached nearby at 916 feet.

Unlike many villages on the walk, Shap is not jigsaw material, but a working village based on the local stone. Much in evidence are the granite works and limestone quarries near the village. With it's pinkish hue, the Shap granite is particularly popular, being much-used in public buildings. Historically, Shap's one building of interest is the Market Hall, which is almost 300 years old.

Market Hall, Shap

The Market Hall can be found in the centre of the village, on the west side of the main street.

| DAY TWO | | SHAP TO POOLEY BRIDGE |

Distance — 13½ miles

Going — easy

Highest point — Heughscar Hill, 1231 feet

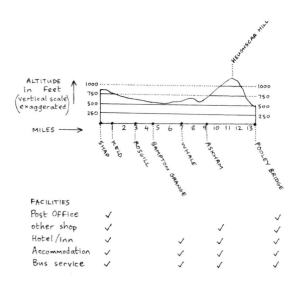

FACILITIES

	SHAP		KELD	ROSGILL	BAMPTON GRANGE	WHALE	ASKHAM		POOLEY BRIDGE
Post Office	✓								✓
other shop	✓						✓		✓
Hotel/inn	✓				✓		✓		✓
Accommodation	✓				✓		✓		✓
Bus service	✓				✓		✓		✓

From Shap the Way heads over fields to the two religious houses of Keld Chapel and Shap Abbey before arriving at the River Lowther. The river remains in close proximity for several easy miles to pass through Bampton Grange and later the grounds of the ruinous Lowther Castle. A long but well-graded climb leads from the river, through Askham village and on to the open moor. The top of a grand little fell is visited before a steady descent to finish.

SHAP to KELD

Route

Leave the main road through Shap by a lane on the left just next to the Fire Station. It leads onto a back street, West Close, which runs parallel with the A6. Turn left along it, then almost immediately go through a gate on the right, from there following a walled track to another gate. Go through it, leaving the last of the houses behind to reach the top of a gentle rise from where the High Street range, Lakeland's eastern skyline, comes into view.

The steady descent to Keld is punctuated by a variety of stiles built into the veritable labrynth of limestone walls hereabouts. After negotiating two stiles a field is entered containing a large standing stone, and the exit is into a grassy snicket. Take the stile in front, heading away from the snicket and keeping left of a collapsed wall. From the next stile go forward to two prominent trees: on reaching them ignore the gate into the lane, but continue instead to the bottom of the field.

Disregard a stile in the wall on the right in favour of one in the very corner, here entering another large field. Stay with the wall on the right, almost to the bottom corner, where an unobtrusive little stile deposits you into the lane as it prepares to enter Keld.

Keld is a tiny hamlet by the River Lowther, on the end of a mile-long cul-de-sac. The Chapel dates back to the 16th century, and is thought to have belonged to Shap Abbey. It is now in the care of the National Trust, and it's basic interior can be viewed by obtaining the key from the cottage across the road.

Of ancient origin, this is one of a long line of such stones which point north-west from a stone circle south of Shap. Several of the others can still be located, though not from our route.

Route

The lane is left after only a few yards by a stile adjacent to a gate on the right. Pass to the right of a converted barn, and when the accompanying wall turns sharp right go straight ahead to another wall-corner. Crossing a collapsed wall, continue ahead with a wall now on the left, locating an easily-missed stile very cleverly built into it. Once over, go right to a stile and continue on the level to another stile: the proud tower of Shap Abbey appears in the valley bottom, and can be reached by simply dropping down to the left (At the bottom, take the right-hand track over the old bridge, not the more direct private farm road).

From the vicinity of Hegdale, the long, low line of Knipe Scar can clearly be seen ahead and to the right

Having inspected the ruins climb back up the unenclosed road as far as the lone dwelling on the left, there taking the two gates at it's top side. Head along the bottom of this and the next field, beyond which a track leads to the farm buildings ahead. Of the several choices available, take the gate-way on the left of the main building and make for the gate at the far end, doing likewise across the bottom of two fields. Now aim half-right to a stile in a wall-corner, with a more dilapidated one just beyond. Aim now for the narrow gap between the houses just in front, with nettles and a ruinous stile proving to be obstacles before emerging onto the lane through Rosgill.

Cross the lane to a stile just to the left in the opposite wall, then head straight across the field to locate a narrow stile. A large field is entered: slope diagonally across to the far bottom corner, using a telegraph-pole as a guide. From the gate there, turn right along a farm-road to reach Hegdale. Do not enter the cluster of buildings, but continue along the good track towards a barn. A stile to the right of it admits into a large field, through which a tractor-track heads to the far end. From the stile there, our way continues through lush riverside pastures.

Like Keld before it, Rosgill is a tiny community of farms and cottages, flanking a lane leading down to the River Lowther.

The River Lowther flows for sixteen miles, every one of which is within Westmorland's borders. From being born out of the reservoir in appropriately-named Wet Sleddale to losing it's identity in the Eamont near Penrith, it's grassy banks bear no witness to industrialisation. Indeed, Bampton Grange is the only community through which it flows.

Strange then, that the only real sign of interference by man is at the very outset, in the modern dam that plugs what was once an unspoilt valley.

Rosgill

River Lowther

Shap Abbey

On passing through the gates by this house, the Lake District National Park is entered. Our route remains within it for almost five days.

Shap Abbey
Westmorland's only abbey stands well hidden in an idyllic riverside location. The tower is the obvious focal point, presiding over the otherwise low-lying ruins. Much of the stone is built into the adjoining farm. Well worth a visit: admission free!

Keld

Route

Cross the small stream and the stile and head off again through the field. After crossing the far wall by a stile, a curious little by-way is entered, which seemingly leads from a barn down to the river. We use it, however, only to reach a stile opposite: from it follow the river yet again. Leave the field by a prominent stile in the far wall, then aim for a wicket-gate to enter the churchyard. Leaving by another gate on the other side of the graves, the road through Bampton Grange is joined.

Turn left as far as the bridge, then right along the Bampton road as far as the bridge over Haweswater Beck. Immediately after, use the wicket-gate on the right to rejoin the River Lowther. This we follow upstream through a succession of stiles on a grassy embankment as far as an impressive-looking suspension bridge. Cross this wooden structure which is guarded by a gate at each end and caters solely for pedestrians; given dodgy conditions, it's crossing can be quite exhilarating. From it, head half-right across the rising moor, which is a little damp under-foot, and aim for the prominent telephone-box which presides over a junction of lanes.

Use the gate to leave the T-junction on the lane signposted to Whale. After an initial steep pull, follow this quietest of by-ways for about three-quarters of a mile, then watch for a track heading away to a barn on the right. Here leave the road, but instead of using the track, opt for the stile just through the gate.

typical local roadsign at Knipe junction

From the stile head down the middle of this large field, leaving it by a wooden stile in the bottom right-hand corner. Now slope down to the beck beyond to cross by a stone slab footbridge. Rise straight up the field behind, and bearing just to the left of the house directly in front, a small gate will be found adjacent to it. It empties onto a lane about to enter Whale.

The RIVER LOWTHER to LOWTHER PARK

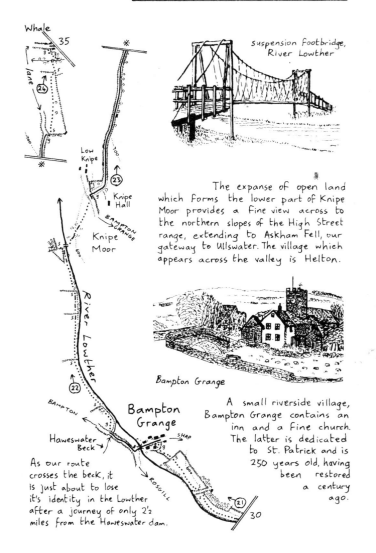

suspension footbridge,
River Lowther

Whale

Low Knipe

Knipe Hall

BAMPTON GRANGE

Knipe Moor

River Lowther

BAMPTON

Bampton Grange

Haweswater Beck

SHAP

ROSGILL

The expanse of open land
which forms the lower part of Knipe
Moor provides a fine view across to
the northern slopes of the High Street
range, extending to Askham Fell, our
gateway to Ullswater. The village which
appears across the valley is Helton.

Bampton Grange

A small riverside village,
Bampton Grange contains an
inn and a fine church.
The latter is dedicated
to St. Patrick and is
250 years old, having
been restored
a century
ago.

As our route
crosses the beck, it
is just about to lose
it's identity in the Lowther
after a journey of only 2½
miles from the Haweswater dam.

Askham

Askham has often been described as the most attractive village in Westmorland, a title to which it certainly makes a good claim. It is a sizeable village, stretching from the church, stood in isolation down near the river, to the breezy heights on the very edge of the moor. The green is of extensive proportions,

Askham Bridge

sloping through the lower half of the village. It is at it's best in springtime, when hordes of daffodils add further colour to supplement the whitewashed cottages flanking the green.

The finest building hereabouts is the Hall, home of the Lowther family: it is stood well back to the right as we enter the village. In parts it dates back to the 14th century, and incorporates various later additions. The Church is a mere 150 years old, and was designed by the same Mr. Smirke who created Lowther Castle. The Lowther name is a part of Westmorland's history: their first knighthood came in 1640. A fire destroyed the original castle in 1720, and the present building, dating from 1811, is now only a shell itself. From a distance however, it's magnificent size totally belies it's derelict state. The vast grounds hold an excellent old

St. Peter's, Askham

church, an estate village, a wildlife park and a deer park. The horse-trials are a popular annual event, and the Lowthers still contribute much to Cumbrian life.

It may come as a surprise to find Askham is within the National Park, for due to it's position it has survived as a part of rural Westmorland, and has avoided the excesses of the gift shop world of the Lakes village. Long may it continue to do so.

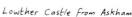

Lowther Castle from Askham

During the long trek up through Askham, pause for a look back across the valley to the impressive array of turrets and towers of Lowther Castle.

Arrival at Askham Bridge signals the end of our friendship with the River Lowther

From the fork in the path a detour can be made to the Castle, but a high wall around it's perimeter results in the building not being seen to good effect.

LOWTHER

POOLEY BRIDGE PENRITH

Hall

26

Inn

Inn

HELTON BAMPTON

37

Askham

River Lowther

Lowther Park

Bartree Scar

highly prominent in the walk through the park

25

Whale Farm

33

Whale

Route

Turn right into the tiny settlement of Whale, which is all but surrounded by the extensive Lowther grounds: after only a few yards take a stile next to a gate on the left. Follow the wall away to another stile at the far end. Entering a large field, keep to the right, passing farm buildings to arrive at a stile 30 yards past a gate. Over this stile the grounds of Lowther are entered: turn left on a good estate path.

The river soon returns to provide company again, though more often than not it is obscured by trees. Our wide track passes through several gates until when the river departs in style through a minor gorge, it climbs to enter woods via a cattle-grid. After a level section it soon rises again: here we fork left on an inviting grass avenue through the trees. It makes a gradual descent towards the river, and emerges onto a road adjacent to Askham Bridge. Cross it and climb the road up into Askham: on eventual arrival at a staggered road junction, continue up the lane beyond.

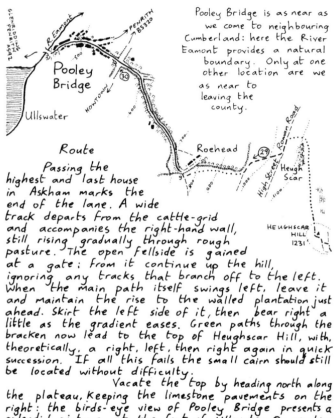

Pooley Bridge is as near as we come to neighbouring Cumberland: here the River Eamont provides a natural boundary. Only at one other location are we as near to leaving the county.

Route

Passing the highest and last house in Askham marks the end of the lane. A wide track departs from the cattle-grid and accompanies the right-hand wall, still rising gradually through rough pasture. The open fellside is gained at a gate; from it continue up the hill, ignoring any tracks that branch off to the left. When the main path itself swings left, leave it and maintain the rise to the walled plantation just ahead. Skirt the left side of it, then bear right a little as the gradient eases. Green paths through the bracken now lead to the top of Heughscar Hill, with, theoretically, a right, left, then right again in quick succession. If all this fails the small cairn should still be located without difficulty.

Vacate the top by heading north along the plateau, keeping the limestone pavements on the right: the birds-eye view of Pooley Bridge presents a splendid picture at the foot of Ullswater. On reaching the top of the limestone cliff of Heugh Scar, incline down the grass slope beyond to the conspicuous line of the High Street Roman Road. Turn left along it beneath the scar, then after only a short distance take a right fork to descend to a wall-corner. Now leave this path and accompany the wall down, bearing left to a gate to the left of the farm buildings at Roehead. Here the fellside is left and the head of a lane joined: follow it all the way down, straight across a crossroads and into Pooley Bridge.

NOTE : IF the weather should be atrocious on departing
Askham, the path-less section over Heughscar Hill
can easily be omitted by staying on the main path
across Askham Fell instead of continuing up to the
plantation. On arriving at a
boundary post (inscribed 'SH MH 1727'),
turn right on a well-blazed path
to descend to Roehead

CROSS FELL   LITTLE DUN FELL   GREAT DUN FELL

The highest
Pennines from
Heughscar
Hill

35

27

Pooley
Bridge

29

Askham Fell

Pooley Bridge is a tidy
little village standing at the
very foot of Ullswater. It's
name comes from the splendid
stone structure that spans the Eamont almost immediately
after it's emergence from the lake Built almost entirely on
the southern side of the bridge, the vast majority of the
buildings line the main street. North of the village rises
the conspicuous wooded hill of Dunmallet, at the foot of
which is a pier for the Ullswater steamers.
          A regular service operates between here
and Glenridding at the head of the lake, breaking it's
journey midway, at Howtown. It may be noticed that
it's course coincides with tomorrow's route, but thoughts
of taking the soft option should be firmly disregarded,
not least of all because the pier is in Cumberland!
          The River Eamont is very much like the
Lowther in that it starts life full-grown and has avoided
industrialisation. It later merges into the River Eden.

DAY THREE   POOLEY BRIDGE TO PATTERDALE

Distance — 12¼ miles

Going — moderate

Highest point — Arthur's Pike, 1747 feet

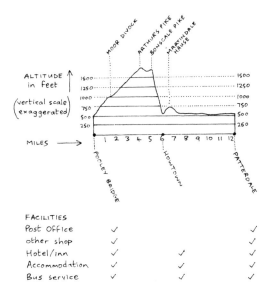

FACILITIES

Post Office	✓		✓
other shop	✓		✓
Hotel/inn	✓	✓	✓
Accommodation	✓	✓	✓
Bus service	✓	✓	✓

     By the end of today's walk Ullswater, England's second largest lake, will have become a firm friend, for both it's proximity and it's beauty dominate the day. From Pooley Bridge the route first returns to the moor, then makes one of the most gentle ascents in the district to Arthur's Pike via an impressive stone circle. It's twin Bonscale Pike precedes a steep descent to Howtown, and after a look at Martindale the lakeshore is followed all the way to Patterdale.

NOTE: As the map indicates,
Howtown is only four
miles distant by road
and if the departure
from Pooley Bridge be
marred by low cloud
on the hills, then this
alternative should be
seriously considered.

Pooley Bridge

Route

Leave Pooley Bridge the
way it was entered, re-tracing
steps back up the lane as far
as the gate onto the open fell.
From it head straight up the
wide stony track which rises
at a gentle gradient
across the moor. After
about three-quarters
of a mile, a large
cairn is reached. At
this junction fork right
on a level, rather damp
path which leads direct
to the surprisingly
extensive stone circle.

Between the large cairn
and the stone circle, our
route again follows in
the steps of the Romans,
for this is part of their
famous road linking the
forts at Ambleside (GALAVA)
and Brougham (BROCAVUM).
Known as the High Street,
it reaches it's highest point
at 2700 feet on the fell
that now bears it's name.

The moorland
track out of
Roehead is
often crawling
with pony-
trekkers from
the local
centre.

The Cockpit (with Blencathra
in the far distance)

Moor
Divock

Cockpit Stone Circle

Route

At the stone circle our path reaches a T-junction. Turn right along it (left if joining it from the circle) on a good path which contours along to the deep confine of Aik Beck. At the wall-corner just beyond, leave the main path and head half-left up a pleasant grass path between bracken. At a fork take a narrower grass strip to the right: in parts sketchy it rises to reach a large cairn. From it head for a similar cairn visible further up the hill, on a delightful path which initially remains near the steep drop to the right. The summit cairn of Arthur's Pike now appears directly ahead, and is soon reached on an equally pleasant path.

The view is excellent, but can be improved further by walking north from the summit to locate the cairn illustrated here. In view is Ullswater and the Helvellyn range

ARTHUR'S PIKE
1747'

The next objective, Bonscale Pike, is in view from Arthur's Pike but from this angle it resembles anything but a pike, higher ground rising almost immediately to the left of it.

BONSCALE PIKE — 1718'

Swarthbeck Gill

35

Howtown

43

Mellguards

Fusedale Beck

36

Swarthbeck Gill is NOT recommended as an alternative descent.

The hinterland of Arthur's Pike is home for a large number of fell-ponies, grazing semi-wild.

From Aik Beck the main path begins a gradual descent to Howtown, thus providing another 'escape-route' should weather conditions deteriorate.

Route continued

From the summit of Arthur's Pike head south, past a crumbling wall (of value as a shelter) and a lesser cairn to pick up a sketchy path. After only a short distance take a right fork to descend to a prominent ruined sheepfold by Swarthbeck Gill. To the left of the fold are stepping-stones, from where the grassy slopes behind rise to the tiny cairn which marks the summit of Bonscale Pike. Once again a fine cairn to the north provides a superb vantage point, particularly for a birds-eye view of the Howtown area.

The foot of Ullswater from the aforementioned stone man. From below it stands on the horizon, looking like the summit.

To reach Howtown, scotch any ideas of a bee-line, instead following a very sketchy path south from the summit. The way remains almost level for a considerable distance, and the temptation to descend the steep fellside should be avoided until a dry, grassy gully appears ahead. Slope down to it to join a cairned path, which after descending in zig-zag fashion, doubles back across the fell on a well-engineered grass ledge. Before long it turns left to drop more steeply to the intake-wall. Go left to a gate into the drive of Mellguards, and after a few steps down it take a stile on the left to a stone-slab footbridge over Fusedale Beck. Just up the slope behind is a farm-road: Howtown is only two minutes down the lane to the right. If no refreshment is needed, simply head up the slope behind the farm-road.

Route

Climbing the grass slope alongside a wall, a clear path soon materialises as the initial steepness subsides. Rounding the foot of the rugged ridge descending from Steel Knotts, a marvellous green rake curves around the hollow of The Coombs to level out before swinging right to emerge onto an unenclosed road by a church: this is Martindale Hause.

Turn left along the road for a few yards only, then as it begins to descend fork right on a sketchy, level path to a stile in a wall. Cross the two fields behind, each time to a stile adorned with a small gate. From the latter a clear path, still on the level, heads through bracken to a gate. A walled track now leads past the dwelling of Hallinbank to another gate: descend the large field to the nearside bottom corner, where a wicket-gate will be found between beck and barn. A path runs alongside the beck to a stile in front of the house at Bridgend. Turn left along the drive which bridges Howe Grain Beck and Boardale Beck in quick succession, to emerge onto the lane leading into Sandwick from Howtown.

St. Peter's, Martindale Hause

Follow the lane to the right, leaving it on a well-blazed path to the left as the lane begins to descend to Sandwick. Accompanied by an intake-wall, this popular path calls for few instructions: shortly after leaving the environs of lively Scalehow Beck the wall is left behind, and here commences a walk in heaven.

HOWTOWN to ULLSWATER

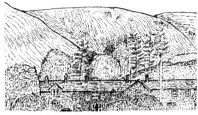

The Howtown Hotel

The name Howtown is somewhat misleading for there is no town here, in fact only a hotel and a few cottages. The hotel is a homely place with a public bar well-hidden round the back, a tiny room that looks as it must have done forty years ago.

Howtown Wyke is a small bay that sees plenty of action in the summer months from a variety of craft. A little pier serves to break the journey of the Ullswater steamer.

Martindale Hause, more usually known as just 'The Hause', links Martindale with Howtown and the outside world. The church which stands on the very summit is only a century old, replacing the much older St. Martin's further up the dale. If at all possible a detour to the ace viewpoint of Hallin Fell (1271') is a must. Only 15 minutes up the path opposite the church.

Secluded Martindale is seen to perfection shortly after leaving The Hause. The main valley is that of Howe Grain, formed by the meeting of Bannerdale and Rampsgill, deep in the Martindale deer forest. The whole area is generally known as Martindale Common.

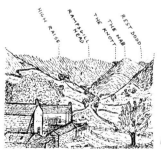

Martindale from Hause Farm

Ullswater is the shapeliest of Lakeland's many sheets of water, having a dog-leg bend which effectively divides the lake into what have become known as it's three 'reaches'. The lower reach covers the first miles from Pooley Bridge, in what are relatively pastoral scenes. The middle reach heads past Howtown towards Glenridding, and becomes increasingly dominated by

M.Y. Raven, Ullswater

the fells. The shorter third reach to the head of the lake is then totally overshadowed by mountains

Patterdale

Patterdale is the undisputed 'capital' of the Ullswater valley, standing at the very head of the lake in the wide green strath of the Goldrill Beck. It is a tiny place, with it's various components spread along the A592 road. 'St. Patrick's Dale' is an extremely popular resort, but due to it's lack of size has thankfully not reached the over-commercialised situation of other central lakes villages.

Although Patterdale is almost completely hemmed in by mountains, a motor-road manages to escape in two opposite directions. The only level exit is to the north, where the road clings to the western shore of the lake to foil the steeply-descending fells. The other option is to the south, where a first-class road climbs high over the Kirkstone Pass to connect Patterdale with Windermere and Ambleside. Almost choked with coaches in the high season,

the pass reaches a height of 1479 feet, and squeezes between mountains a further thousand feet higher. On the very top can be found the second highest inn in the country, once known as the 'Traveller's Rest' for fairly obvious reasons.

Goldrill House, Patterdale YHA

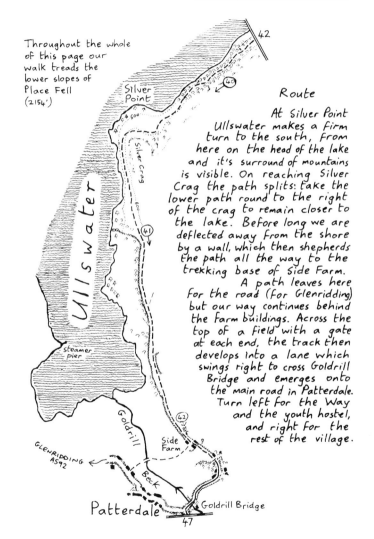

Throughout the whole of this page our walk treads the lower slopes of Place Fell (2154')

Route

At Silver Point Ullswater makes a firm turn to the south, from here on the head of the lake and it's surround of mountains is visible. On reaching Silver Crag the path splits: take the lower path round to the right of the crag to remain closer to the lake. Before long we are deflected away from the shore by a wall, which then shepherds the path all the way to the trekking base of Side Farm.

A path leaves here for the road (for Glenridding) but our way continues behind the farm buildings. Across the top of a field with a gate at each end, the track then develops into a lane which swings right to cross Goldrill Bridge and emerges onto the main road in Patterdale. Turn left for the Way and the youth hostel, and right for the rest of the village.

DAY FOUR   PATTERDALE TO GRASMERE

Distance — 9¼ miles

Going — moderate to strenuous

Highest point — Fairfield, 2863 feet

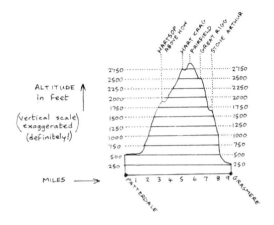

        This is the half-way stage in every
context: the descent from Fairfield exudes a
strong feeling of having rounded the turning
point. This section is devoted entirely to the
mountains, and if the weather conditions are
bad or even dubious at the outset, then unless
these fells are well-known an alternative route
to Grasmere should be taken. The obvious and
best is the bridle-path over the Grisedale Hause,
a direct walk clearly shown on the O.S. map
but still an exhilarating yet safe trek through
the hills, even in low cloud.
        The main route is an excellent fellwalk
that remains on the mountains for all but a
mile at each end. The lack of miles is more
than compensated for by the terrain.

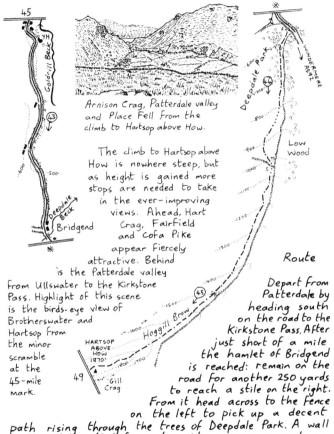

PATTERDALE to HARTSOP·ABOVE·HOW

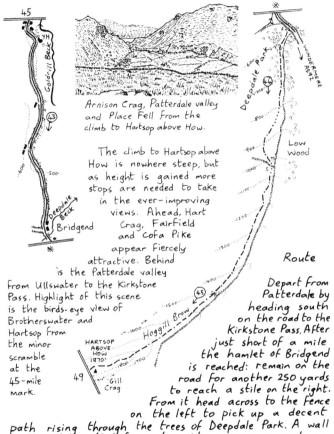

Arnison Crag, Patterdale valley and Place Fell from the climb to Hartsop above How.

The climb to Hartsop above How is nowhere steep, but as height is gained more stops are needed to take in the ever-improving views. Ahead, Hart Crag, Fairfield and Cofa Pike appear fiercely attractive. Behind is the Patterdale valley from Ullswater to the Kirkstone Pass. Highlight of this scene is the birds-eye view of Brotherswater and Hartsop from the minor scramble at the 45-mile mark.

Route

Depart from Patterdale by heading south on the road to the Kirkstone Pass. After just short of a mile the hamlet of Bridgend is reached: remain on the road for another 250 yards to reach a stile on the right. From it head across to the fence on the left to pick up a decent path rising through the trees of Deepdale Park. A wall soon replaces the fence to guide us ever upwards on what is still a broad ridge. After being rather sketchy, the path picks up again beyond a stile in an intervening wall. When the wall finally departs, our ridge is now a good deal shapelier, and the modest summit cairn is a mere five minutes distant on almost level terrain.

Route

From the summit of Hartsop above How continue along the ridge, dropping slightly to a wet depression before beginning a gradual rise towards Hart Crag. As the climb becomes steeper and the ridge less broad, do not err left towards a depression on the main ridge but follow a line of cairns up a steep, stony gully to the right (these cairns are much less solid than they once were). Continuing uphill through an extensive field of boulders, the path can easily be lost: however simply head directly up the slope and the summit cairn of Hart Crag will soon be located. It is set back a little from the main path along the ridge.

In good conditions the path can be abandoned in favour of the rim of the crags from the vicinity of Greenhow End to the top of Fairfield

Having reached the main ridge we can now take advantage of the fact by including further tops in the day's walking for little extra effort. From the cairn return to the main ridge-path which heads north to shortly descend to a grassy col. Climbing away from it in zig-zag fashion through a stony area, the path soon swings left along the broad eastern shoulder of Fairfield, through short-cropped turf providing easy walking. In part cairned, the path soon bends right to approach the highly prominent summit of Fairfield, highest point of the Westmorland Way.

A few notes on Fairfield appear opposite

Helvellyn group from Fairfield

key to illustration

Hart Crag is second only to Fairfield in the heights our walk takes in, and is just as rugged as it's master. As is the case with virtually all lakeland fells, the mighty crags hover over the northern and eastern coves. Here is one of the finest.

HARTSOP ABOVE HOW 1870'   47
1800

46

Link Cove

HART CRAG 2698'
1500
47

Hartsop above How is a fell in exactly the same form as several others that rise from the valley floor near the foot of Kirkstone Pass. All are intermediate summits part-way up ridges that continue to rise much higher still. It forms an upthrust on the ridge which gives a false impression of independance when viewed from the valley bottom. The parent fell, in this case, is of course Hart Crag.

As already mentioned, Fairfield's top is the summit of the walk, and at 2863 feet above sea level it is the second highest mountain entirely within Westmorland, being overtopped only by Catstycam, a lesser-known peak in the Helvellyn range. Also of greater height are Helvellyn itself and Bowfell, but these two giants are shared with neighbouring Cumberland.

The top of Fairfield is an interesting place. Although almost completely surrounded by grass, the immediate environs of the summit are strewn with rocks and overpopulated with cairns. The summit cairn is deservedly the most substantial, whilst to it's north-east is a sprawling stone shelter. Only yards from here is the abrupt north-eastern terminus of the extensive summit plateau, from where Fairfield's mighty cliffs plunge into Deepdale. The top of the gully nearest the summit is often the haunt of Fairfield's last patch of snow: don't lean too far over looking for it though, we're only half of the way to Arnside.

shelter ← gully
summit cairn
old shelter
short row of stones
→ From Hart Crag
to Great Rigg
SUMMIT PLAN

Route

The next objective is Great Rigg, the summit due south along the ridge. From the cairn head away from the steep drops to north and east, instead passing the small row of stones on the summit plateau: Great Rigg is in view directly ahead, in front of the shimmering lake that is Coniston Water. On leaving the stony terrain behind, the ridge begins to narrow and a clear path materialises. After dropping down to a slight depression, a gentle five-minute climb is made to Great Rigg's summit cairn.

Continue south from the top, passing a subsidiary cairn before dropping through low outcrops to another cairn. Here our way leaves the main ridge, branching right along the broad but well-defined arm that leads unerringly to Stone Arthur. Arrival at the top will not be in doubt, for having passed by some outcrops the steady descent is halted by the abrupt end of the ridge.

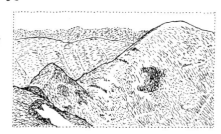

Cofa Pike and St. Sunday Crag from Fairfield

The Fairfield Horseshoe

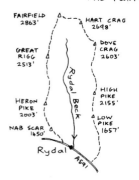

Fairfield stands at the head of the valley of Rydal Beck, and sends a high ridge down each side of it. One culminates abruptly near Rydal, while the other descends more gently almost to Ambleside. The traverse of these two ridges is the highly popular Fairfield Horseshoe: the terrain is conducive to striding out, and allows eight summits to be 'bagged' in one day's relatively easy walk.

Our route takes in three of the four major tops.

FAIRFIELD to STONE ARTHUR

Aside from pages 80/81, the walking contained
on this page is the easiest to be
found on the Westmorland Way.

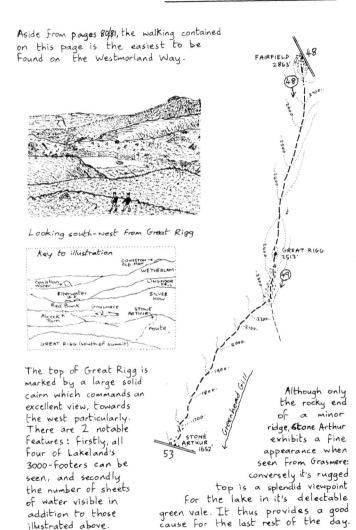

Looking south-west from Great Rigg

Key to illustration

The top of Great Rigg is
marked by a large solid
cairn which commands an
excellent view, towards
the west particularly.
There are 2 notable
features: Firstly, all
four of Lakeland's
3000-footers can be
seen, and secondly
the number of sheets
of water visible in
addition to those
illustrated above.

Although only
the rocky end
of a minor
ridge, Stone Arthur
exhibits a fine
appearance when
seen from Grasmere:
conversely it's rugged
top is a splendid viewpoint
for the lake in it's delectable
green vale. It thus provides a good
cause for the last rest of the day.

Grasmere

Grasmere is famous on two counts, firstly for it's natural beauty and also for it's literary connections. The village stands in a verdant vale through which flows the River Rothay before it empties into Grasmere. Like Patterdale it has a surround of high fells, but here they do not impose quite so much, opting to provide a less intimidating background. Although the village centre is only small, there are several outlying hamlets which throw in their weight. These settlements are strung along the main Windermere to Keswick road, which thankfully avoids the village centre.

It is in one of these hamlets, Town End, that stands the house they all come to see: here is Dove Cottage, home, if only for a short while, of the one and only William Wordsworth. In actual fact, the highly — esteemed poet never knew it by that name, but he lived here, and that is what attracts the many thousands of visitors that come each year. A converted barn across the road serves as a Wordsworth museum. The village also contains two of his later residences, though neither are open to the public. One of these is the Rectory, across the road from the Parish Church of St. Oswald.

Dove Cottage

Inside this very church-yard Wordsworth now rests, the grave being marked by the most plain of headstones: he lies surrounded by his family and friends. Also buried close by is the Arctic explorer, Sir John Richardson. The church itself appears rather basic from the outside, for the stone structure of the tower is hidden under a layer of rough-cast, the function of which is to protect the old tower from the elements. The interior is splendidly simple, with many dark beams exposed to contrast well with the gleaming white-washed walls.

Grasmere's own sheet of water stands away from the village and in contrast remains relatively quiet. It's only traffic is the rowing boats available for hire. Grasmere's annual Sports are famous throughout the land, the one-day event comprising all the traditional sports and entertainment.

STONE ARTHUR to GRASMERE

Route

Leave Stone Arthur by a path departing from the top in the direction of Grasmere. It becomes immediately steep as it drops between rock outcrops, but then eases for a while before resuming the gradient to descend through a gap in a wall. On next meeting a wall, turn right to follow it's level course through the bracken. When it drops down to a plantation, turn left alongside it to begin what is positively the last descent, steeply again, to the tumbling waters of Greenhead Gill.

Do not cross the bridge, but go through the gate on the right and head down the tree-shrouded lane. At a junction turn left to soon emerge onto the A591 adjacent to the imposing Swan Hotel. Cross straight over and head down the lane into the centre of Grasmere

51
STONE ARTHUR
1652'
50
1600
1500
1400
1300
1200
1100
1000
900
800
700
600
500
400
300
Greenhead Gill

Keswick A591

51

AMBLESIDE A591

River Rothay

local celebrities

Grasmere

55

Standing on the very summit of Helm Crag, the Lion and Lamb are popular landmarks that have caused centuries of travellers to lift their eyes upwards

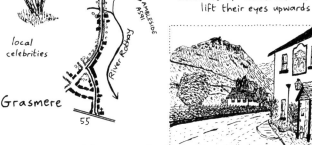

The Lion and Lamb from the Swan Hotel

| DAY FIVE | | GRASMERE TO TROUTBECK |

Distance — 11¾ miles

Going — moderate

Highest point — Silver How, 1292 feet

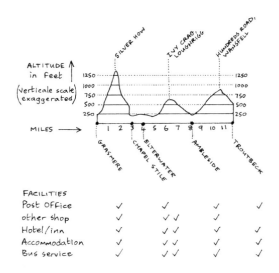

FACILITIES

	GRASMERE	CHAPEL STILE	ELTERWATER	AMBLESIDE	TROUTBECK
Post Office	✓		✓	✓	✓
other shop	✓	✓	✓	✓	
Hotel/inn	✓	✓	✓	✓	✓
Accommodation	✓	✓	✓	✓	✓
Bus service	✓	✓	✓	✓	✓

This day's walk through central lakeland connects two popular valleys and finishes in a third. The major climbing comes at the outset, when the beautiful fell of Silver How is traversed to reach the Langdale valley. Both the tiny lake of Elterwater and Skelwith Force are visited before crossing the slopes of Loughrigg to return to the Rothay valley at Ambleside. The last stretch takes in the noted viewpoint of Jenkin Crag to follow an old bridlepath to Troutbeck.

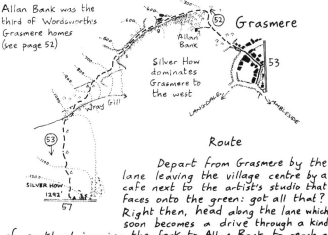

Allan Bank was the third of Wordsworth's Grasmere homes (see page 52)

Silver How dominates Grasmere to the west

Route

Depart from Grasmere by the lane leaving the village centre by a cafe next to the artist's studio that faces onto the green: got all that? Right then, head along the lane which soon becomes a drive through a kind of parkland, ignoring the fork to Allan Bank to reach a farm. Use the gate to the left and follow the rising path which becomes enclosed for a while before emerging via a stile onto the open fell.

Now a steepish climb ensues, to enter an area thick with juniper: several unnecessary cairns point the way, but shortly before emerging from the trees watch for a left fork in the path, indicated by two small but important cairns. The path leads to Wray Gill, turning to follow it upstream. Soon it crosses the fairly deep ravine to the gentler slopes opposite. After a few sketchy yards the path becomes clear again, and at a cairn the summit appears. An easy trek leads straight to it (steeply at the end).

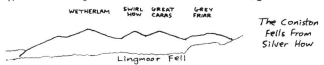

The Coniston Fells from Silver How

Silver How is one of Lakelands more beautiful fells; although of modest altitude it stands proudly in the centre of things, dividing the popular valleys of Langdale and Grasmere, and thus giving fine views. The summit cairn stands near the steep Grasmere edge.

Route

Leave the shapely summit cairn by heading south: after only a few yards a large cairn should be seen ahead about a quarter-mile distant, and it is the key to the descent to Langdale. Aim directly for this cairn on a sketchy path, the cairn temporarily escaping from view. On reaching it, continue a little further to the south to drop down to join a level path: turn left along it, rounding a corner to arrive at a sprawling cairn at another junction of paths. Turn right (south again) and within a few steps a grooved path develops to enter the rugged territory of Megs Gill.

The upper ravine with it's tumbling falls is negotiated and after a while on the opposite bank the path contours away from the beck's confines. Ignore a path branching steeply left and remain on the level until the next fork left. This path descends rather steeply and crosses a small beck to the interesting environs of the disused Thrang Quarry. Now composed entirely of discarded slates, the path runs between walls of slate, and yards before reaching the top edge of the quarry itself it turns sharp left to become a track debouching onto a back lane in Chapel Stile.

Turn left to the junction by the church and then right to join the main road. Follow it left to the large hotel, after which take a footbridge on the right to cross Great Langdale Beck. Turn left on a path which climbs to join a quarry road when the spoil heaps give way to trees. Followed down to the left it emerges directly next to the bridge in Elterwater village. Cross it and turn right into the car-park, at the far end of which a gate precedes a well-used path parallel with the beck.

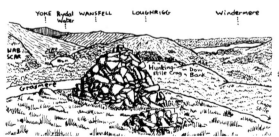

East-south-east from the big cairn above Megs Gill

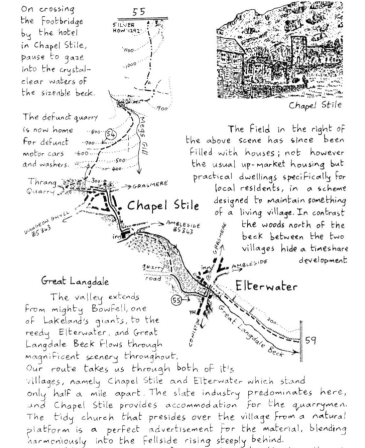

On crossing the footbridge by the hotel in Chapel Stile, pause to gaze into the crystal-clear waters of the sizeable beck.

The defunct quarry is now home for defunct motor cars and washers.

55

SILVER HOW 1292'

Chapel Stile

Chapel Stile

The field in the right of the above scene has since been filled with houses; not however the usual up-market housing but practical dwellings specifically for local residents, in a scheme designed to maintain something of a living village. In contrast the woods north of the beck between the two villages hide a timeshare development

Great Langdale

The valley extends from mighty Bowfell, one of Lakeland's giants, to the reedy Elterwater, and Great Langdale Beck flows through magnificent scenery throughout. Our route takes us through both of it's villages, namely Chapel Stile and Elterwater which stand only half a mile apart. The slate industry predominates here, and Chapel Stile provides accommodation for the quarrymen. The tidy church that presides over the village from a natural platform is a perfect advertisement for the material, blending harmoniously into the fellside rising steeply behind.

Elterwater receives far more tourist attention than it's near-neighbour, due to it's tiny sloping green complemented by a whitewashed inn, and the undulating bracken-covered common just north of the village. Both draw throngs of visitors, for beer in the sun and equally-relaxing picnics, respectively.

Route

As Great Langdale Beck nears the shore of Elterwater, our path continues on into the trees. We eventually arrive at the lakeshore almost at it's foot, on emerging from the wood where the well-blazed path ends. After having paused to appreciate a neatly-framed view of the Langdale Pikes, head across the open meadow, keeping the outflowing River Brathay well to the right. At the end of the field everything converges at a gate, and a good path through the trees accompanies the narrowing and increasingly wild river to Skelwith Force. By now the road is running parallel, and the path soon emerges onto it behind the hotel at Skelwith Bridge.

Here the Langdale road meets the main Ambleside-Coniston road, but happily we escape this busy junction immediately by heading up the steep lane to the north. It soon levels out to arrive at a T-junction: take the right arm over a small beck, then leave it within yards along a metalled farm-road left. As it approaches Tarn Foot do not enter it's confines but turn along a track to the right. At a gate continue ahead, up a short slope to a gate onto the open fell. A pleasant grooved path remains close to the intake-wall then climbs a little to arrive at a memorial seat under the shadow of Ivy Crag. This well-sited seat will entice all to sit and gaze at the outstanding Brathay scene.

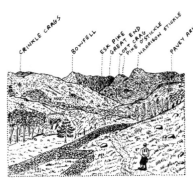

Langdale from the path
below Ivy Crag

ELTERWATER to IVY CRAG

The green, Elterwater

The tarn to which Tarn Foot refers is Loughrigg Tarn, a modest sheet of water to the north of the farm. It is partially visible during the climb to Ivy Crag

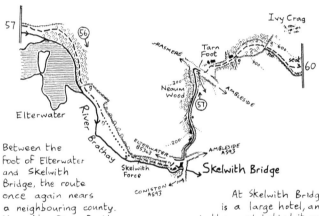

Between the foot of Elterwater and Skelwith Bridge, the route once again nears a neighbouring county. Here the River Brathay provides the boundary, and the adjoining county on this occasion is Lancashire.

At Skelwith Bridge is a large hotel, and in the yard behind it can be seen a showroom for the local slate products.

The main feature here though is Skelwith Force, a waterfall whose lack of height is more than made up for by it's ferocity: a substantial amount of water has to be forced through what is only a narrow rock passage.

Langdale Pikes from Elterwater

Route

From the seat below Ivy Crag the path turns in a north-easterly direction, and the wall soon departs at a right-angle. Go straight ahead, ignoring any lesser deviations to arrive at the small Troughton Beck: beyond it the path rises a little to pass between gentle slopes to reach a gate. The descent to Ambleside begins here: across some rough pasture the path improves greatly to pass the clubhouse of the former golf-club. Becoming a wide track, the way descends more steeply to Brow Head, where it receives a layer of tarmac before dropping to a minor road in the valley bottom.

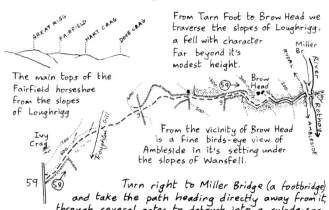

The main tops of the Fairfield horseshoe from the slopes of Loughrigg

From Tarn Foot to Brow Head we traverse the slopes of Loughrigg, a fell with character Far beyond it's modest height.

From the vicinity of Brow Head is a fine birds-eye view of Ambleside in it's setting under the slopes of Wansfell.

Turn right to Miller Bridge (a footbridge) and take the path heading directly away from it, through several gates to debouch into a cul-de-sac. At the main road turn right into Ambleside centre. Our way goes straight through as far as the traditional-looking White Lion Hotel on the left: soon after take the Old Lake Road to walk in peace above the busy main road.

Just short of their re-union, take a wide track on the left, rising steeply and twisting before a good level part with fine views of Windermere. Skelghyll Wood is entered and we climb again to cross a beck. At the end of the next short climb a sign announces arrival at Jenkin Crag, and a path to the right leads onto the top of the Crag itself.

Miller Bridge

Ambleside

One of the Lake District's major centres, Ambleside obviously relies heavily on tourism, but still not quite to the extent of, say, Bowness: although the streets are thronged with holidaymakers and hotels and guest-houses abound, there remains a strong air of self-respect. There are still many houses without the almost obligatory 'B+B' signs in the window and still one or two unspoilt local hostelries.

Most visitors manage either a game of putting or a stroll down to Waterhead for a sail on Windermere, while others simply settle for taking a snap of the popular Bridge House. This fascinating structure is a tiny two-storeys astride Stock Ghyll: even the stairs are outside. It now houses a National Trust information room.

Other notable features are the church with it's graceful spire, Stock Ghyll Force, and the Lake District History Centre, all of which are handily placed. In a field at Waterhead, a mile south, are what remains of 'GALAVA', a Roman fort. This key position at the head of Windermere ensures Ambleside's popularity and importance.

GRASMERE A591

60

KIRKSTONE

Bridge House

Ambleside

A591

LAKE ROAD

A591

61

WINDERMERE A591

a sign of local tradition, in evidence in Ambleside.

The Bridge House

Skelghyll Wood

63

Jenkin Crag

HARTLEY'S ULVERSTON

BEER FROM THE WOOD

Route

After rejoining the main path from the Crag, press on through the wood: at a gate the trees are left behind and the farm of High Skelghyll looms just ahead. Enter by the gate in front, passing between the buildings and out via the farm's access road at the far side of the yard. It descends to a cattle-grid and a bridge: here leave it by a gate on the left, straight after the bridge. A good path slopes up the field by a fence, passing a ruined barn and swinging in to cross a small beck. It continues through two fields, and at the second gate the enclosed track known as the Hundreds Road is joined.

Here our crossing of this historic route to Troutbeck reaches it's highest point: not only is it all downhill from here on, but it impossible to go astray. Turn right along the track, and ignoring two other enclosed ways descending to the right, it will lead us unerringly into Troutbeck. We join the road adjacent to the institute and post office: youth hostellers and those continuing the walk should turn right, otherwise go left into the 'centre' of the village to seek accommodation.

Troutbeck

A long, narrow village, Troutbeck stretches for more than a mile from the Queens Head at Town Head, south to Town End. Each of these extremities boasts an interesting building: the attractive old inn includes a 'four-poster bed' bar amongst it's features, while at Town End stands a superbly-preserved example of a statesman farmer's house from the 17th century. The house is owned by the National Trust and is open to the public.

Between these two outposts a succession of farms and cottages cling to the narrow lane: there is no depth at all. Strangely the church stands aloof, tucked away on the main Windermere-Patterdale road, parallel with the village but a half-mile distant.

Townend

JENKIN CRAG to TROUTBECK

Windermere from
Jenkin Crag

The National Trust
sign, complete with
alternative spelling

Jenkin Crag has long been one
of lakeland's most renowned viewpoints,
firmly in the tradition of the 'viewing
stations' of the first tourists. For
today's tourists it is still the end of
the road, and most will re-trace their steps
back to Ambleside or Waterhead.

Troutbeck has a lesser-known namesake
in Cumberland, on the
Keswick-Penrith road.

From leaving
Skelghyll Wood to
joining the Hundreds Road,
the views south and west
are superb. The most striking
feature is undoubtedly England's
largest lake, for a substantial
length of Windermere can be
seen. The tarn on it's far bank
is the little-known Blelham Tarn.
Less appealing are the 'cardboard
huts of the water-ski centre at
Low Wood, nearer to our feet.

On reaching the Hundreds
Road, turn to see the mountains
at the head of Langdale, with
the Pikes as inspiring as ever.

The Hundreds Road is
an old track leading up to
higher pastures Known as
the Troutbeck Hundreds. The
name dates back centuries
and refers to the division
of rough grazing land on
the higher slopes of Wansfell,
the mountain whose slopes
we have trod since Ambleside.

DAY SIX		TROUTBECK TO KENDAL

Distance — 16'4 miles

Going — moderate

Highest point — Scout Scar, 764 feet

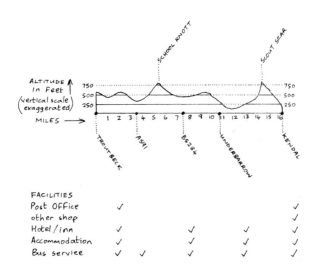

FACILITIES

Post Office	✓				✓
other shop					✓
Hotel/inn	✓		✓	✓	✓
Accommodation	✓		✓	✓	✓
Bus service	✓	✓	✓	✓	✓

Busy lakeland is now left behind. From Troutbeck, field-paths are mostly used to approach the attractive fell of School Knott, above Bowness. From there rough uplands and more field-paths are taken to reach the Underbarrow valley. The final pull of the day is a short, steep one to the escarpment of Scout Scar. A fine walk along the edge is followed by a gradual descent to Kendal.

Route

From the Post Office follow the road south out of the village. At Townend ignore the turn-off to Ambleside and continue down the lane to the last houses. Here an enclosed track descends to the left to cross Trout Beck by two wooden bridges. Beyond, the path climbs through a large field to join the main road at a gate. Turn right for 350 yards (footpath provided) to locate a wicket-gate on the other side. From it a pleasant grass rake slopes halfright across the field, crossing a small beck before arriving at the farm buildings at the opposite side.

Using a stile between these buildings go forward to a crossroads of minor lanes, then straight across on a tarmac farm-road: it leads unerringly to Far Orrest Farm. Now avoiding the farmyard, take a wicket-gate on the left just before the first building, and aim diagonally across the field to another gate. Take yet another in the wall just behind, then follow this wall right to reach a fourth gate emptying onto a walled track.

The Troutbeck fells from near Townend (left to right)
Thornthwaite Crag
Froswick
Ill Bell
Yoke

Route

Once on the track beyond Far Orrest, all the farm buildings are left behind. Do not however follow the track, but go through a wicket-gate opposite to enter a field. Follow a tractor-track across towards a gate, but use a stile a few yards to it's left. Bear half-left across the next field to a stile, from there heading along the left of a field to a stile in the wall-corner. Ahead is Near Orrest farm: aim straight for it, one more stile being met on the way. On reaching the buildings take the gate on the right, followed by two more in quick succession to cling to the outer edge of the farm. The third gate deposits us at the front of the large farmhouse, from where a right turn leads out onto a lane.

Turn left along this quiet lane as far as a crossroads, then right along a similar narrow lane to emerge onto the main Kendal to Windermere road. Cross at once to the footpath on the other side, then turn right only as far as the first gate. Entering a field, follow a tractor-track to a gate at the far end, doing likewise in the next field. At this second gate take a stile alongside to enter a different field, there following the dividing wall away. When it is replaced by a fence, a white stile will be seen ahead: use it to cross the railway line (here within a mile of it's terminus) to a twin stile on the opposite side.

From the railway stile, follow the fence sloping down in front to a stile in the corner. Behind it a small beck is crossed to the drive of the large house on the left, which goes by the modest title of Sheila's Cottage. Turn down the drive to a junction near a little stone bridge embowered in trees. Head up the lane to the left alongside the modern housing development on the outskirts of Windermere.

Once through a gate, head up the open field to the left to reach a stile in the top-left corner. This admits to the open fellside, and the top of School Knott will be gained in under ten minutes by simply aiming for the highest point. There is no clear path, but neither is there need for one.

Near Orrest

The seat at this minor crossroads is well-sited, for it commands an excellent prospect of the Coniston and Langdale fells

The farmstead of Near Orrest is a marvellous old building in the form of an immense L-shape

On the long section of lane from the seat to the A591, the wooded hill across to the right is Orrest Head. It is a popular tourist objective and viewpoint, being close to Windermere railway station.

The Kendal to Windermere road is one pulsating highway, being the most regular route of entry into the central Lake District.

The single-track Kendal and Windermere Railway was opened in 1847, due mainly to the efforts of one Cornelius Nicholson of Kendal. When his town was left high and dry by the construction of the main line two miles to the east, he successfully campaigned for a branch line which, in the end, went all the way through to Windermere. At the time only a hamlet existed there, but the town of Windermere soon materialised to complement Bowness down by the lake.

One of the line's greatest critics was none other than Mr. Wordsworth, who feared that it would bring thousands of town and city folk flooding into his unspoilt Lakeland: one consolation was that plans to extend it to Ambleside were shelved. It is ironic that although visitors come in far greater numbers than Wordsworth could have imagined, only a handful use the rail to Windermere.

The Lakeland skyline from School Knott

From west to north (approx.)   Distances in miles

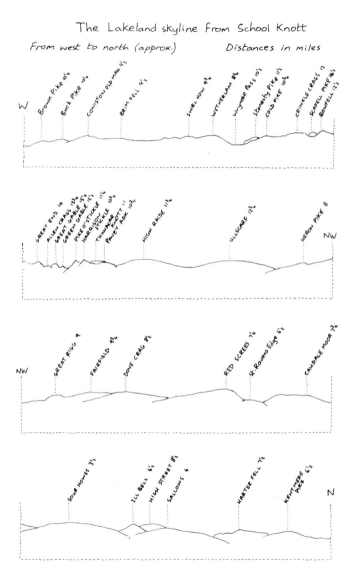

SCHOOL KNOTT to GILPIN BECK

Route

Leave School Knott's appealing summit by heading south-east towards School Knott Tarn, this attractive sheet of water already being in view. Cross the intervening wall by a conspicuous stile and make for the water-edge, there turning right to the outlet. Accompany the tiny beck down to a gateway in the parallel wall, from here doubling-back half-left through the bracken on a very sketchy path to arrive at a junction of collapsed walls. Bear right, away from the junction on a good, level path which soon swings left to skirt a marshy area on it's left. Through heather, bracken and a gateway the path continues, to eventually descend slightly to a stile in a solid-looking wall directly ahead. From it aim for the buildings ahead, crossing a ruinous wall on the left to go round the back of the first building. A gate between the two buildings gains entry to the farmyard of Hagg End.

Leave the farm by it's access-road to join a narrow lane: the amount of rusting machinery hereabouts almost merits description as a farm museum. Turn right to round a corner to the farm buildings of Outrun Nook, then take a wicket-gate opposite the cottage. Aim straight up the centre of this large field, bearing left to a gate in the wall at the top end. Keeping the wall on the left a track is joined and Crag House appears across to the right. Remain on the track which swings left to some gates: take the right-hand one. When the wall turns left, remain on the track to descend more gradually to the infant Gilpin Beck. A sketchy path by the beck leads to a wall, crossing it, and then the beck, before continuing.

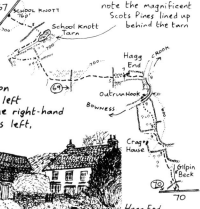

67 SCHOOL KNOTT 760'

School Knott Tarn

note the magnificent Scots Pines lined up behind the tarn

Hagg End

CROOK

69

Outrun Nook

BOWNESS

Crag House

Gilpin Beck

70

70

Hagg End

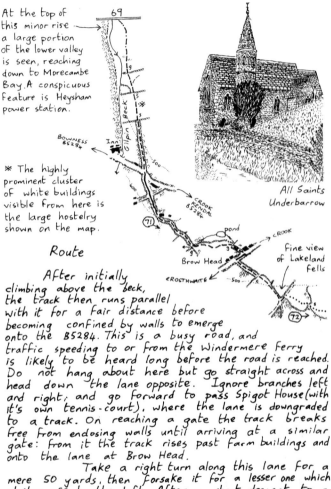

At the top of this minor rise a large portion of the lower valley is seen, reaching down to Morecambe Bay. A conspicuous feature is Heysham power station.

✳ The highly prominent cluster of white buildings visible from here is the large hostelry shown on the map.

All Saints Underbarrow

Route

After initially climbing above the beck, the track then runs parallel with it for a fair distance before becoming confined by walls to emerge onto the B5284. This is a busy road, and traffic speeding to or from the Windermere ferry is likely to be heard long before the road is reached. Do not hang about here but go straight across and head down the lane opposite. Ignore branches left and right; and go forward to pass Spigot House (with it's own tennis-court), where the lane is downgraded to a track. On reaching a gate the track breaks free from enclosing walls until arriving at a similar gate: from it the track rises past farm buildings and onto the lane at Brow Head.

Take a right turn along this lane for a mere 50 yards, then forsake it for a lesser one which strikes off to the left. After a short descent to a cattle-grid, this farm-road climbs steeply to a junction of tracks: here leave it by turning sharp-left to enter a large field. Aim half-right across this field to locate a stile just past the gate in the far top

Route continued

corner. In the next field stay close to the fence on the right to leave by the second gate reached. A decent track now heads up the hill to pass through two gates in quick succession. As the corner is rounded the farm buildings of Low Fold appear ahead, and the track duly leads straight there via more gates.

Pass straight through the farmyard and out onto the access-road. On emerging from enclosure by walls it turns left: here abandon it by going ahead to drop through a gateway to arrive at a stile through the bottom corner of the field. Now pathless, continue down to another stile to enter an immense pasture. With no path to follow, aim across the intervening dip keeping closer to the right-hand wall. At the brow of the slope opposite, bear away from the wall to locate a step-stile in a fence barring our way. From it a path descends steeply through profuse bracken to join an enclosed track.

Follow it for 40 yards to the right, then take the first gate on the left. A path heads away from it alongside a wall on the right, remaining with it to cross a little beck before descending via a gate onto a lane. Turn left for a short distance then take a gate set back slightly on the right. Head away alongside a wall, to locate a stile at the far end, then continue by a hedge to another stile. Beyond it cross a stone slab, rounding the left side of a grassy mound: a wicket-gate leads to a stile onto the road beneath Underbarrow Church.

Low Fold

On rounding this corner the long line of Scout Scar appears ahead, our final obstacle of the day.

The environs of Underbarrow are at their best in spring, when the well-known damson display is outstanding

(73)

CROOK

←Underbarrow

Lane

CROSTHWAITE← Broom Farm

72

Route

Set off right along the road, but where a lane doubles back to the left, leave it in favour of the enclosed track immediately in front. When the track forks, take the left branch opposite a cottage, and stay on it till it rejoins the road. Turn left along it, passing through more of the village to a junction near the inn: turn right here, then left almost at once down another lane. After just under half a mile take a stile on the left to rise to another stile, then a gate. Pass between a private house and it's garage to follow the drive down onto a lane.

Turn left along the lane, past Tullythwaite House and over a slight rise to find a gate on the right where the wall gives way to a fence. Squeeze through a stile next to it and head straight across the field to a stile in a tiny section of wall. From it aim half-right to a stile by a gate in the far top corner of the next field, then head for a small barn on a mound, passing to it's right to find a gate onto a lane.

Head left down this lane as far as the first buildings on the left, there taking a track on the right towards two houses. Pass to the right of them, through a stile, then as the track fades head left across the pasture to rise to a gate in the wall there. The dense woodland of Barrowfield Lot is immediately entered. A good path heads away from the gate in winding fashion: avoid any lesser branches to emerge into a clearing of thick bracken. At the far end of this clearing a steep bank confronts us: do not struggle up it but deflect to the right to re-enter the trees. Now in fine fettle, the path heads through the dark confines, crossing at right-angles two other paths in quick succession before arriving at a stile in a wall. Emerge from the wood into a large field, crossing the dip in the centre to a stile at the highest point opposite. A rough path climbs through a narrow cluster of trees to another wall, and from the stile there a short scramble leads up to Barrowfield.

Turn right on the track in front of the farm buildings, and then sharp left to go round the

Route continued

back and into the farmyard. Turn right after the first barn to a gate, from where a track climbs up the field behind the farm. When it swings left at the top, break off right to a gate into the woods. Now at it's very foot, Scout Scar presents a formidable obstacle, but the climb on a good path is less of a trial than was anticipated. On gaining the top at a cairn, go left along the crest of the scar on a pleasant path near the edge (with a closer variation if required!). The long march to the shelter is eased by the nature of the terrain, the view, and the special satisfaction of gaining this landmark which has been in view for much of the day.

Scout Scar from Underbarrow

The limestone escarpment of Scout Scar is a major feature of south Westmorland and a prime objective for fortunate Kendalians. The highest point is marked by a unique shelter, a 'mushroom' which incorporates an extremely well-restored view indicator. Though the extensive lakeland fells naturally dominate, our eyes may well be diverted south, to Arnside Knott.

Underbarrow is an attractive village nestling in a vast rural area: it has no definable centre, it's buildings being scattered in all directions. Apart from the inn, all it's needs are met in Kendal, 3 miles distant.

Kendal

By far the largest town in Westmorland, and the administrative centre, Kendal is affectionately known as the old grey town, a description it lives up to when seen from the vicinity of the by-pass. The town has long been known for it's snuff and woollen cloth industries, and more recently shoe production. The main street is a hive of activity, being lined with shops and inns throughout it's length. It's northern end, Stricklandgate, received publicity in 1824 when it was the first road in the country to be endowed with a layer of 'tarmac', courtesy of a Mr. MacAdam.

Running parallel with the street is the River Kent from which the town takes it's name, and it's course through the centre of town is the reason for several fine bridges. Though Kendal seems busy enough now, it was, until the construction of the western by-pass, a horrendous bottleneck. Standing as it does at the convergance of the A65 with the A6, it was required to funnel hordes of visitors through it's main street from the two most popular routes of entry into lakeland.

The town has much of interest and merits a far more leisurely exploration than our whistle-stop permits. History abounds, from the splendid Museum of Lakeland Life and Industry in the Abbot Hall, to the real thing, including the Castle ruins, the Castle Dairy, and a lot more, particularly in the main street with it's countless old yards. The church is claimed to be the country's oldest parish church.

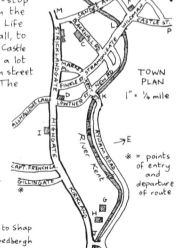

TOWN PLAN

1" = ¼ mile

☀ = points of entry and departure of route

A - Railway station B - GPO
C - Bus station D - Town Hall
E - Castle F - Castle Dairy
G - Abbot Hall H - Parish Church
I - Brewery Arts Centre and Y.H.A.
J - Nether Bridge K - Miller Bridge
L - Stramongate Bridge
  all other buildings omitted
M - B5284 to Windermere N - A6 to Shap
O - A685 to Appleby P - A684 to Sedbergh
Q - A65 to Settle R - A6 to Milnthorpe
  all minor roads omitted

Fisher's Tenement

73

On reaching the Brigsteer road the Way finally leaves the National Park after 60 consecutive miles, a sequence that began way back at Shap Abbey.

Kendal's main street is our old friend the A6, also last encountered at Shap

Route

Leave the shelter by heading south on a path just behind it. Almost immediately a lesser path branches left off it, gradually making for the near-parallel wall where a narrow kissing-gate will be located. On lovely turf a path heads directly east for Kendal, passing through another kissing-gate before joining the farm-road from Fisher's Tenement (note the site of the old racecourse). On reaching the road turn left to bridge the by-pass before dropping into Kendal. On reaching a junction turn right to descend Gillingate onto the main street. (see plan opposite)

A locally-made delicacy, consumed in enormous quantities on all the best expeditions

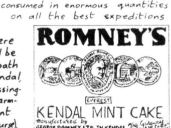

Nether Bridge and All Saints Parish Church

| DAY SEVEN | | KENDAL TO ARNSIDE |

Distance — 18¼ miles

Going — easy

Highest point — Arnside Knott, 521 feet

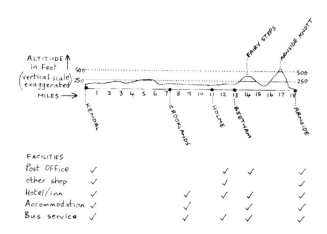

FACILITIES

	Kendal						Crooklands				Holme	Beetham					Arnside
Post Office	✓									✓	✓					✓
Other shop	✓									✓						✓
Hotel/inn	✓						✓			✓	✓					✓
Accommodation	✓						✓			✓	✓					✓
Bus service	✓						✓			✓	✓					✓

This final day is also the longest, but the nature of the terrain ensures easy walking. From Kendal the River Kent is accompanied for several miles, and on leaving it the Way heads for more water in the form of the Lancaster Canal: it's towpath is trod for several miles further with much of interest. After passing the inspiring Farleton Knott and the uninspiring M6 motorway, the canal is finally abandoned at the village of Holme, and tiny old Beetham is soon reached. Woodland paths lead to the hilltop Fairy Steps, from where a descent to Hazelslack with it's pele tower is followed by a final climb, to Arnside Knott. It is then all downhill to the Kent estuary, and Arnside.

Route

To leave Kendal follow the road south out of town from the Parish Church, crossing the road bridge (Nether Bridge) soon reached and continuing in the same direction. Parted temporarily from the river by a factory, it is rejoined near a suspension footbridge where the main road heads away from the river. Here forsake that road for a lesser one to remain parallel with the nearby riverbank.

After dragging on for some time past housing and the endless works of that well-known footwear company, the last house on the left is reached: on our right a footpath sign points the way through a gap in the low wall and a little unconvincingly into a factory car-park. Enter it and turn left after the building to pass between the works and the river. As the car-park ends the way narrows between warehouse and trees: press on to reach a stile, and a little beyond is another which empties onto the road to Watercrook.

Turn right to pass through a gate, and after a few yards leave the farm-road and head half-left across the field to join the bank of the river, now in much more convivial surroundings. The way to Hawes Bridge is now simple: although the path is not always evident we simply follow the river, taking in a variety of stiles before emerging through trees onto the lane near the bridge. Turn right down to the bridge, but instead of crossing it take a stile on the left, to follow the trees to a stile before descending to rejoin the river.

Kendal

River Kent

sewage works

Watercrook

NATLAND

River Kent

Inside the large loop of the river at Watercrook is the site of a Roman fort, 'ALAVNA'.

❋ note the start of a mill-race on the opposite bank – the ruined mill is just above the bridge

SIZERGH ← →NATLAND

Hawes Bridge

peer over this odd-shaped structure to see the river in a rocky gorge

75

80

46

5.R.

Fb

79

Route

A good path accompanies the river now, taking in several more stiles and often separated from the Kent by trees. After merging with a bridleway we emerge into a large riverside pasture, crossing it to reach the bridge in sight at the far end. Negotiate this rather hairy suspension bridge which spans the Kent at what seems to be the widest possible point, and turn left on a tarmac farm-road running parallel with the river. At a junction with a lane stay alongside the river to arrive at a larger T-junction, here turning down to the left to a wide road bridge over the Kent.

At the far side of the bridge we now say farewell to the Kent by taking a stile just across the road, and head straight up the field to a kissing-gate. Cross the minor road there to a twin gate opposite, and head straight up the field to a redundant bridge over the drained Lancaster Canal with which we shall soon be on more intimate terms. Above the bridge a large field is entered: climb alongside the fence on the left to the brow of the hill and then drop down to a gate onto a narrow lane.

As with the previous lane, use it only to reach the other side, where a stile deposits us into another field. Head up alongside a fence, crossing an intervening stile before descending to the railway line: it is flanked by a stile at each side and needs to be crossed with care as it is the main west-coast line to Scotland. From the stile on the other side, turn sharp right to a stile in a wall, crossing it and then following the wall away from the railway line. This accompanying wall is superceded by a fence, which deflects us to the right around a right-angle before reaching the field corner. Two adjacent stiles are encountered here, one in the fence on our left and one in the fence just met (the two can be negotiated without touching the ground between). While stumbling over them, console yourself with the fact that there are no more for several miles. Now head up alongside a hedge to emerge via a gate onto a lane.

Turn right along this narrow by-way and, enclosed by fine hedgerows, follow it for half a mile to descend to cross a bridge over what is now the northern terminus of the Lancaster Canal. Use the stone steps to reach the towpath, and head off along it.

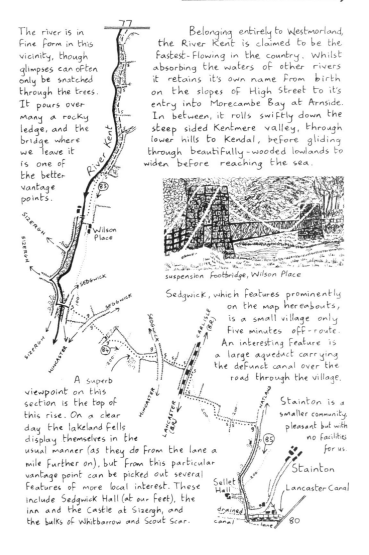

The river is in fine form in this vicinity, though glimpses can often only be snatched through the trees. It pours over many a rocky ledge, and the bridge where we leave it is one of the better vantage points.

Belonging entirely to Westmorland, the River Kent is claimed to be the fastest-flowing in the country. Whilst absorbing the waters of other rivers it retains it's own name from birth on the slopes of High Street to it's entry into Morecambe Bay at Arnside. In between, it rolls swiftly down the steep sided Kentmere valley, through lower hills to Kendal, before gliding through beautifully-wooded lowlands to widen before reaching the sea.

suspension footbridge, Wilson Place

Sedgwick, which features prominently on the map hereabouts, is a small village only five minutes off-route. An interesting feature is a large aqueduct carrying the defunct canal over the road through the village.

A superb viewpoint on this section is the top of this rise. On a clear day the lakeland fells display themselves in the usual manner (as they do from the lane a mile further on), but from this particular vantage point can be picked out several features of more local interest. These include Sedgwick Hall (at our feet), the inn and the castle at Sizergh, and the bulks of Whitbarrow and Scout Scar.

Stainton is a smaller community, pleasant but with no facilities for us.

Stainton

Lancaster Canal

Route

Although the whole of this section is along the Lancaster Canal, all is not quite as straightforward as might be reasonably expected. All is well until just after Millness Bridge: here the canal comes up against the formidable opposition of the M6 motorway. Naturally the waterway is the loser, having been given the chop in the name of progress. Pass round the end of the water onto the road under the motorway, then immediately back to the re-instated canal. At the next bridge but one the canal is once again bisected, but this time a narrow concrete tunnel is provided for foot-travellers.

At Duke's Bridge we leave the canal to avoid another impasse a little further on (the M6 again). The bridge is best identified by the large basin that precedes it: climb the steps after the bridge and follow the road away from the junction. After bridging the motorway take a gate on the left to walk parallel with it to return to the tow-path via a gate. After one more bridge the hapless canal is again split, this time by a lesser road. Stiles at each side link the two pieces of water. The canal is left for the last time at the next bridge but one: climb the steps to it and descend the farm-road into Holme village.

Crooklands is the only place of refreshment between Kendal and Holme. Conspicuous on the hilltop behind is the church of St. Gregory.

Oldhall Bridge

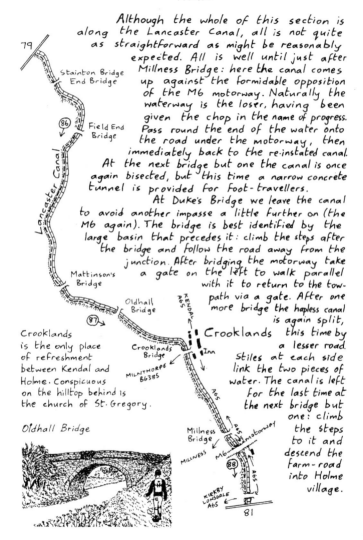

79

Stainton Bridge End Bridge

86

Field End Bridge

Lancaster Canal

Mattinson's Bridge

Oldhall Bridge

87

Crooklands Bridge

MILNTHORPE B6385

Crooklands

KENDAL A65

Inn

A65

Millness Bridge

MILLNESS

M6 motorway

A65

88

KIRKBY LONSDALE A65

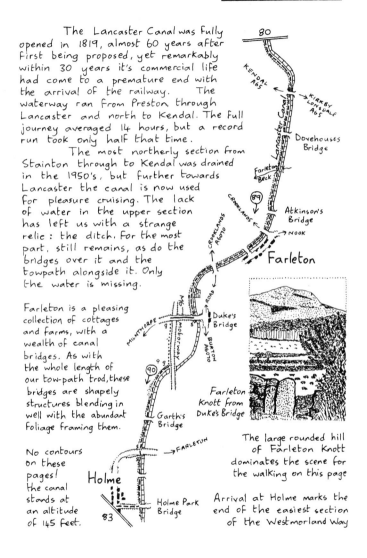

The Lancaster Canal was fully opened in 1819, almost 60 years after first being proposed, yet remarkably within 30 years it's commercial life had come to a premature end with the arrival of the railway. The waterway ran from Preston, through Lancaster and north to Kendal. The full journey averaged 14 hours, but a record run took only half that time.

The most northerly section from Stainton through to Kendal was drained in the 1950's, but further towards Lancaster the canal is now used for pleasure cruising. The lack of water in the upper section has left us with a strange relic: the ditch. For the most part, still remains, as do the bridges over it and the towpath alongside it. Only the water is missing.

Farleton is a pleasing collection of cottages and farms, with a wealth of canal bridges. As with the whole length of our tow-path trod, these bridges are shapely structures blending in well with the abundant foliage framing them.

No contours on these pages! the canal stands at an altitude of 145 feet.

Farleton Knott from Duke's Bridge

The large rounded hill of Farleton Knott dominates the scene for the walking on this page

Arrival at Holme marks the end of the easiest section of the Westmorland Way

Route

On joining the road through the village of Holme turn left for about 200 yards then leave it where a footpath sign on the right points the way to Beetham through the gate of Paddock Lodge. Go straight ahead past some stables to a gate, and then on again to a stile by a gate. Cross a small enclosure to another stile just ahead and, finally free of the farm, go ahead again to a gate across the field. A tractor-track is followed away from it for a few yards, but when it leaves the field continue to a gate in the far corner. Squeeze through a gap-stile next to it and the way is now straightforward; with a hedge on the left pass along the edge of three fields to emerge onto a lane. Cross straight over to a stile and then head across the field to a stile onto the main railway line once again. From the stile on the other side head directly away to a gate; from the stile by it use another to enter the field on the left. Accompany the dividing fence up the slope before dropping to a lane.

this track by the barns is likely to be rather muddy

ARNSIDE

MILNTHORPE

Beetham

R. Bela

SILVERDALE YEALAND

Beetham Hall

CARNFORTH RD

85 Underlaid Wood

Fairy Steps

Arrival at the Fairy Steps is like suddenly reaching the end of a long, dark tunnel. It also signals the start of the last stage of the walk, almost all of which is within the fine view, along with the south lakeland fells.

The 'steps' themselves are a narrow cleft in a limestone cliff, much-used in the past as a short-cut to Beetham church, and also of course, as legend would have it, by the fairies!

The final miles: Arnside Knott and Arnside from the Fairy Steps

HOLME to the FAIRY STEPS

Route continued

Turn left along this lane, past the buildings of Pyes Bridge Farm to a gate on the right: a sign points the way half-left to the top of the field, and from the stile in the hedge there aim for the grouping of large barns directly ahead. A gate before them precedes a rough track out onto the A6. Cross to the footpath and turn right, soon leaving it for the Beetham turn-off. In the village, round the corner by the hotel and head along the lane between it and the church. After the last house take a stile on the left to climb straight up this large field to a stile into the woods. Turn left on a path which swings right to join a wider path. Turn right along this to a gate, after which fork left on a rising path to eventually come to a 'crossroads'. Head straight on up to soon emerge at the top of the Fairy Steps.

Note that the map opposite continues a little past Fairy Steps (route overleaf)

HOLME

CARLISLE (A6)

MILNTHORPE B6384

81

92

Pyes Bridge Farm

HALE

LANCASTER (A6)

B6384

Holme

91

BURTON B6384

Beetham is a tiny greystone village standing safely clear of the busy A6. There are several old buildings around, and the rambling hotel is a welcoming place. Pride of place however goes to the ancient church, whose relative size is due to it's past importance. The tower dates back 8 centuries and appears out of proportion, being a strangely narrow structure. On the edge of the village stands the Hall, a farm incorporating a ruined pele tower.

Holme is another greystone village but with much more modern housing. The village centre is missed by our route, but is worth a detour if time permits. An inn and a shop can be found near the church, which itself is interesting in that it's tower in particular has a similar look to Beetham's.

St. Michaels, Beetham

Route

After admiring the view from the Fairy Steps, locate the obvious split in the cliff and descend the 'steps', which can be quite entertaining with a large rucksack. It is now downhill all the way to Hazelslack: a lesser version of the Fairy Steps is soon encountered, before the good path continues in a straight line and emerges from the wood to pass along the edge of some fields before reaching a lane. Cross over and head along the lane opposite, at once passing Hazelslack Tower.

After 100 yards take a stile on the left by a gate adorned with a caravan club sign, and set off through the field on a broad track which depending on the time of year may be an obstacle course of frisbees and footballs. Just before the track reaches a gate, break off left to a stile in the wall there. A sketchy path heads away from it through rough pasture to emerge via a stile onto a junction of lanes. Turn along to the right, and within 100 yards take a stile on the left: bear right across a curious ditch with some low outcrops to join a farm-track.

Arnside Knott is a rounded limestone hill, cloaked in trees on three sides. It stands like a sentinel watching over the estuary, and indeed the highlight of this far-reaching view is the map-like scene at it's foot, with the mighty viaduct and the houses of Arnside resembling models.

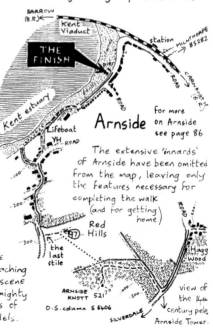

Arnside

for more on Arnside see page 86

The extensive 'innards' of Arnside have been omitted from the map, leaving only the features necessary for completing the walk (and for getting home)

Route continued

Follow this farm-track past a barn and under a railway bridge, then at a multiple-footpath sign turn right to a stile in the field corner. Sandwiched by trees and the railway embankment, the path emerges into a field: head for the farm in front, passing to the left of it and along almost to the road at Black Dyke level crossing. Without setting foot on the road, turn sharp left through a stile by an old gate into Hagg Wood. A good path climbs the edge of the wood, past modern housing which serves to indicate the proximity of our goal. When the gradient eventually eases the path debouches onto an unmade road (Spinney Lane), which itself joins the Arnside-Silverdale road.

Turn left along this road and shortly after disconcertingly leaving behind an 'ARNSIDE' sign, use a gateway on the right to a path straight up through the trees. When it forks left away from the wall, take it to climb to the highest point.

Hazelslack

CARR BANK

82

The ascent of Arnside Knott from the level crossing at Black Dyke is the unkindest 500 feet of all, but worth it!

Dominating the farm of Hazelslack is the ruined pele tower, which despite it's condition and the taming effect of it's foliage still looks mightily impressive. Like many others in the vicinity it was built in the late 14th century to afford protection from the marauding Scots who came this way

BARROW (B.R.)

ARNSIDE

Black Dyke

96

ROAD

Leighton Beck

YEALAND

95

Hagg Wood

note the rather old sign warning of the proximity of a bull

CARNFORTH (B.R.)

Leave Arnside Knott by retracing steps a short distance to the wall to the north: from this best viewpoint use a stile there to descend the large field, bearing left to a stile onto a lane. Turn right down it, passing a junction before an enclosed path on the left leads down onto the front. Turn right along the sand, then a concrete path to Arnside's front: this is it, the end!

Arnside

A bright and breezy place, Arnside stands at the point where the Kent estuary finally gives way to the waters of Morecambe Bay, the massive Kent viaduct providing an arbitrary border. Trains pulling out of Arnside station are on it within seconds, heading for Furness and the Cumbrian coast. This impressive monument to the pioneering railway engineers was constructed in the 1850's, and contains no less than 50 arches.

Arnside is no standard seaside resort, for the attractions, other than natural, are strictly limited. All the important facilities are however readily available, and all the shops display themselves along the seafront. Despite an increasing number of visitors, Arnside remains essentially residential, and behind it's waterfront there sprawls a relatively vast hinterland of suburbia.

The tiny pier was savagely ripped apart by storms in the winter of 1982/83, but has now been restored to first-class condition by virtue of a substantial fund raised mainly by local residents. Just out in the bay the National Park reaches it's most southerly point, between here and Grange-over-Sands, which is three miles distant and clearly visible.

The pier and seafront from the beach

Arnside is a fitting location to conclude a long walk: it provides just the right setting for winding down before having to return home. Find a seat on the front, pier, or better still spread out on the sand (if the tide's out): you can now relax and reflect upon the past week's activities, and later re-live each of those 98 miles in the bar of one of the two hotels on the front. **Cheers!**

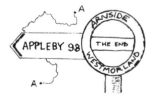

A LOG OF THE WALK

This and the following four pages provide
for a permanent record of the walk

RECORD OF ACCOMMODATION

Date	Address	Comments

RECORD OF THE JOURNEY

When completed, these two pages will provide a permanent record of the walk.

Date	Place	Miles		Times		Comments
		Daily	Total	Arrival	Departure	
	Appleby	–	–			
	Great Ormside	3	3			
	Great Asby	7	7			
	B6260, Bank Moor	10¾	10¾			
	Crosby Ravensworth	12½	12½			
	Shap	16¾	16¾			
	Keld	1¼	18			
	Rosgill	3¼	20			
	Bampton Grange	4¾	21½			
	Whale	7½	24¼			
	Askham	9¾	26½			
	Heughscar Hill	11½	28¼			
	Pooley Bridge	13½	30¼			
	Arthur's Pike	4¼	34½			
	Bonscale Pike	5¼	35½			
	Howtown	6¼	36½			
	Sandwick	8	38¼			
	Patterdale	12¼	42½			
	Bridgend	1¼	43¾			
	Hartsop above How	3¼	45¾			
	Hart Crag	4½	47			

Date	Place	Miles		Times		Comments
		Daily	Total	Arrival	Departure	
	Fairfield	5½	48			
	Great Rigg	6½	49			
	A591, Swan Hotel	8½	51			
	Grasmere	9¼	51¾			
	Silver How	1½	53¼			
	Chapel Stile	2¾	54½			
	Elterwater	3½	55¼			
	Skelwith Bridge	5	56¾			
	Ambleside	8¼	60			
	Jenkin Crag	9¾	61½			
	Troutbeck	11¾	63½			
	A592, near Townend	¾	64¼			
	A591, near Windermere	3¾	67¼			
	School Knott	5	68½			
	B5284, Crook	7¼	70¾			
	Underbarrow	10¾	74¼			
	Scout Scar	13¾	77¼			
	Kendal	16¼	79¾			
	River Kent, near Sedgwick	4	83¾			
	Lancaster Canal, Stainton	5¾	85½			
	Crooklands	7¾	87½			
	Holme	11¼	91			
	Beetham	13	92¾			
	Arnside Knott	17	96¾			
	Arnside	18¼	98			

RECORD OF HOTELS AND INNS VISITED

These two pages should be more than adequate for most thirsts

Date	Inn	Location	Beers sampled	Comments

Date	Inn	Location	Beers sampled	Comments

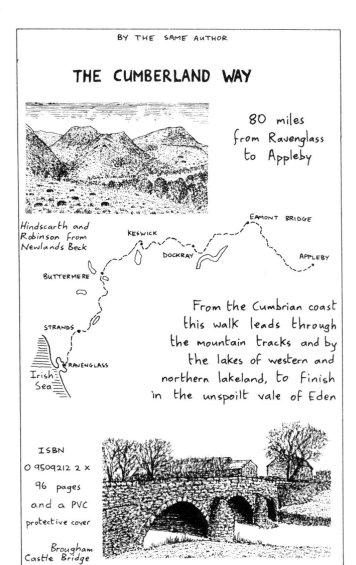

THE CUMBERLAND WAY

80 miles
from Ravenglass
to Appleby

Hindscarth and
Robinson from
Newlands Beck

EAMONT BRIDGE

KESWICK

DOCKRAY

APPLEBY

BUTTERMERE

STRANDS

RAVENGLASS

Irish
Sea

From the Cumbrian coast
this walk leads through
the mountain tracks and by
the lakes of western and
northern lakeland, to finish
in the unspoilt vale of Eden

ISBN
0 9509212 2 x
96 pages
and a PVC
protective cover

Brougham
Castle Bridge

THE FURNESS WAY

75 miles from Arnside to Ravenglass

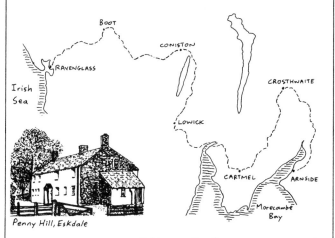

Penny Hill, Eskdale

      This walk of immense variety stretches across the southern Lake District from 'coast to coast'. Between Morecambe Bay and the Irish Sea will be found an area rich in natural beauty and historical interest. From the wide river estuary to the wild mountain pass

ISBN 0 9509212 1 1

   96 pages
and a PVC
protective cover

Cove Bridge, Coniston

INDEX OF PLACE-NAMES ON THE ROUTE-MAPS

INDEX continued